The Decorated Garden Room

The Decorated Garden Room

Interior design for your outside living space

TESSA EVELEGH

Photography by DEBBIE PATTERSON

HH
HERMES
HOUSE

For Jennie

This edition published by Hermes House
an imprint of
Anness Publishing Limited
Hermes House
88-89 Blackfriars Road
London SE1 8HA

A CIP catalogue record for this book is available from the British Library

ISBN 1 84038 246 5

Publisher: Joanna Lorenz

Project Editor: Judith Simons

Text Editor: Maggie Daykin

Designer: Lisa Tai

Photographer: Debbie Patterson

Illustrator: Lucinda Ganderton

Printed and bound in Singapore

5 7 9 10 8 6

PICTURE CREDITS

Camera Press: page 132 bl (Rosemary Weller). The Garden Picture Library: pages 24b (Ron Sutherland); 57 b (Brigitte Thomas); 83 r (Marijke Heuff); 136 (Steven Wooster); 137 tr (Gary Rogers); 139 (Jane Legate). Robert Harding: page 144 b. Jerry Harpur: pages 12 b (designer: Patrick Presto, San Francisco); 32 bl (designer: Keeyla Meadows, San Francisco; 38 b (designer: Sonny Garcia, San Francisco); 101 t (designer: Thomas Church, San Francisco), bl (designer: Cyrille Schiff, Los Angeles); 138 l (designer: Sonny Garcia, San Francisco), r (designer: Vernon Edenfield, Fredericksburg).

Contents

Introduction

There is something very special and satisfying about having your own outdoor space, however small it may be. It is your own little patch of the world to pamper and enjoy without interference (you hope) from anyone else. It is a part of your home that just happens to be outside. And as a part of your home, there is no reason why you shouldn't decorate it in much the same way as you might go about decorating the rooms inside the house.

You can create impact by painting and staining fences, walls, furniture and pots to complement the planting; you can use visual tricks to create perspective and romance; and you can finish it all off with outdoor pictures and decorations. And these are just some of the hundreds of ideas in this book, which I hope will inspire you to think about your garden in a completely different way. You don't need specialist knowledge and you don't have to spend hours toiling to keep it looking good. The aim is to create a delightful living space, craftily organized so that all the family has room to entertain, play or simply relax there.

I do hope you find inspiration from the many pictures, suggestions and step-by-step projects, as you browse through these pages, so you can create an exquisite, personalized outdoor room of your own.

PLANNING YOUR GARDEN ROOM

Transform even the smallest plot into an outdoor room by decorating and furnishing it – in much the same way as you might inside. With everything set out to best effect, it will then be ready for you to enjoy with family and friends at any time.

OPPOSITE: *A simple trellis arbour hung with lanterns, a wooden bench, a table and candlelight create a beautiful outdoor room in which to enjoy summer evenings.*

Major Considerations

The most comfortable and visually pleasing garden rooms are usually the result of careful planning. You will need to consider how best to use the available space, the vista, and the ambience before you prepare the "canvas" for the decorative touches. But once you begin to reap the rewards of such forethought, you will certainly feel it was all very worthwhile.

You will probably want somewhere to sit and, perhaps, eat. If you have children, you will want somewhere for them to play; and you will also need to allow for some kind of storage area for tools, pots and other garden paraphernalia. All this is perfectly possible even in tiny gardens. An area 2m (6½ft) square is sufficient space in which to sit and eat. Children would be thrilled with a sandpit just 1m (3¼ft) square and, if there is just a little more space, there will be room enough for a small play house.

ABOVE: *Even light screening adds interest. Here, a line of neat iris leaves provides a boundary between the patio area and a delightful miniature lawn, lending more importance to both.*

ABOVE: *By dividing up the spaces, you can create visual depth. These two huge box orbs help to define a vista and lend perspective to the arbour at the end.*

RIGHT: *Garden paraphernalia displayed on a delightful wire shelf transforms the functional into the decorative.*

ABOVE: *Low hedging is used here to form visual divides and create several rooms within one garden, for a rich and interesting design.*

Plan out in your mind the best place for each of these activities in much the same way as you might plan your kitchen, where you also need to provide space for working, eating and leisure. Once these priorities are fixed, it will be much easier to work out the layout of the garden. This is important, even if you don't have the resources for new pavings and landscaping, at least for the foreseeable future. For example, there may be a flower bed just where you feel it would be best to create a seating area. With the garden layout left as it is, you would continually have to bring furniture in and out when you need it. That is no more comfortable than a sitting room would be if you had to bring in a chair every time you wanted to relax. However, with a few little changes, like simply turfing over the flower bed, you can organize the garden so it is ready for relaxation any time you want.

Once the main areas are worked out, it is much easier to decide where you want to have planting areas, and within this framework, you will be able to transform the space into a decorative outdoor room that you will want to use for much more of the year than just the few summer months.

Planning for Privacy

You will only be able to relax in the garden once you have organized the basic needs: privacy and shelter. Without the benefit of enclosed spaces, especially in built-up areas, these considerations can be problematic. However, there are ways of achieving them. Trellis can be fixed on top of walls and fences to create extra height. You can then grow decorative climbers to provide a wonderful natural wallpaper. You could plant fast-growing conifers, such as thuja, though check their potential final height or you could end up deeply overshadowed, if not overlooked.

Seating areas in particular need privacy. Even if you live in the middle of the country and have a huge garden, you will feel much more comfortable if you site these where, at least on one side, there is the protection of a wall of some sort. This could be the garden boundary wall, a hedge, or even a trellis screen to lend a more intimate feel. If you are closely overlooked, you may also want to create privacy from above. One of the most successful ways of doing this is to put up a pergola and let it become entwined with vines or other climbers. That way, you have a "roof", which filters the natural light and allows a free flow of fresh air.

ABOVE: *Hinting at secret spaces lends a romantic touch to any garden. This dividing wall hides part of the garden, offering privacy, while at the same time, the archway framing a statue beyond offers perspective to the whole space.*

LEFT: *A Japanese maple, with stunning copper foliage, screens a seating area.*

RIGHT: *Secret places can be created in even the smallest of spaces. This pathway winds through plantings in a tiny 3m (10ft) plot.*

Atmosphere and Romance

Once the space is defined, you can begin to set the mood. Creating ambience relies on stimulating the senses: sight, sound, touch, taste and smell, all of which are supplied free of charge by nature. And simply by being outside, you are closer to nature, so it should be even easier to bring atmosphere and romance to the garden than anywhere else in your home. Stimulating each one of the senses is what this book is all about. The pages are packed with decorative ideas to enhance the garden.

These ideas can be set against the visual delights provided by the plants themselves. As well as the sound of birdsong and buzzing insects, you can add the music of windchimes or the evocative trickling of water in even the smallest plot. The outdoors also provides the most glorious fragrances, both sweet – from flowers such as roses, honeysuckle, jasmine – and aromatic, from lavender and piquant herbs. Touch, too, can be stimulated as it is impossible to walk through a garden without being touched by – or reaching out to touch – some of the plants; this is especially pleasing if they have interesting textures. Plan for a variety of these, including plants whose leaves range from fleshy to frondy and feathery. Finally, eating out in the garden contributes taste to complete the sensory picture.

The most romantic gardens hint at intimacy. They could literally be enclosed outdoor rooms, such as courtyards, balconies or roof gardens, which automatically offer intimacy. If your space is rather larger, you can add romantic interest by creating hidden places. This isn't difficult, even in the smallest garden. You can put a door in the fence or wall to hint at another space; put up an archway to give the feeling of moving from one area to another; or add a trellis screen to section off an eating area, perhaps. As well as creating intimacy, these dividing tactics also create the illusion of space. Adding an archway or screen means you are able to see beyond into another area, which lends perspective to the whole space, giving it structure and shape. However light the resulting screening is, it hints at secret places and romance.

LEFT: *There is nothing more delicious than entertaining al fresco, when fresh seasonal food can be prepared without fuss and the table decorations are delightful in their simplicity.*

RIGHT: *The sound of trickling water enhances any outdoor area, and a water feature need not take up an inordinate amount of space. Water flows elegantly over this exquisite wall-mounted, cast-iron lily pad.*

BELOW: *A miniature courtyard is set out as an enchanting outdoor room. The cherry tree suggests pretty "wallpaper", while the blossom forms a natural carpet. Even a "coffee table" is positioned before the bench and an alcove is set in the wall.*

Finding the Levels

Whereas indoors, generally you would prefer your floor to be level, outside, the opposite is true. This is probably because inside, the various heights of furniture automatically give you interesting levels and furniture tends to occupy a greater portion of floor space. Outside, even furnished gardens offer greater expanses of floor space, which could result in monotony. Unless you have a very tiny space, the proportions of a room inside, or you have decided to have a very particular and probably formal design, such as a knot garden or parterre, you will probably want to create some changes in level.

Even a single step up from one area to another can do the trick. But if you are not in a position to completely re-landscape for the sake of a few levels, there is still a lot you can do. You can add staging at one side, and use that to display potted plants; you can use a plant stand to lend a little height; you can make a feature of garden buildings for higher-than-ground level architectural interest. You can also use plants of various heights to create levels.

ABOVE: *Flowering climbers, such as clematis, don't have to be restricted to walls and fences. By training them up obelisks, you can take the colour even higher.*

LEFT: *Even on a tiny patio area, there is room to create levels. Here, raised beds are built in white-painted brick to match the garden walls.*

OPPOSITE: *A pretty Victorian wire plant stand, filled with flowering plants, brings flashes of white high up in the middle of a largely green planting area.*

Planning the Planting

Herbaceous borders bring wonderful colour in summer but die down to next to nothing in the winter, so it is good to provide an evergreen structure of plants to get you through all the seasons. These can also contribute to the "architecture" of the garden, creating levels, screens, and even sculpture. You can plan to have taller shrubs at the back of the borders, slowly graduating towards the front, or you can make more structured steps. You can arrange rows of small, lightly screening plants across the garden to create a living screen, and you can use specimen trees or neatly trimmed topiary as living sculpture.

The colour scheme can be planned against this basic structure. The decorative garden room is at its prettiest with plenty of colour. The structural shrubs and trees also can be chosen to ensure some colour all the year round – fruit trees for blossom in spring; shrub roses for summer colour; and late-flowering clematis and wonderful berries, such as those of the pyracantha in autumn, and of holly in winter. This display can be complemented by autumn-flowering bulbs such as colchicum, schizostylis and cyclamen.

But the most flexible colour can be added with pots and containers. There is always a choice of seasonal colour at garden centres. By planting up in moveable pots, you can put the colour where you want it, and re-plant with new seasonal colour as the old blooms die down. Pot up bulbs in the autumn in anticipation of spring colour and, as they die down, put them in a secluded part of the garden for their leaves to soak up the light, ensuring a better show next year.

Colour creates much more impact if it is kept to a theme – of blues and pinks, perhaps, or oranges and yellows – and this theme can be strengthened with the use of paint and stain on nearby fences, garden buildings, furniture, or even the pots themselves.

With the introduction of comfortable furniture, and with the finishing touches of accessories and decorations, a garden becomes an outdoor room ready for entertaining and relaxation.

BELOW: *You can use garden flowers outside in the same way as you might use potted plants inside. Here, spring flowers make a charming window display.*

ABOVE: *Conifers tied together at the top make a fabulous evergreen alternative to the classic rose arch.*

ABOVE: *A beautiful specimen plant, such as this rose, makes a delightful feature.*

RIGHT: *Seasonal flowers look lovely potted up and grouped for massed colour. This also allows you to move the colour around the garden whenever you want to.*

FLOORS AND FLOOR COVERINGS

The floor offers the basic structure to the garden room, setting the tone in stone or brick, gravel or grass. And even though these elements may seem fixed, there is still scope for decoration with imagination and flair.

OPPOSITE: *The flooring in this potager-style plot is made up of a system of pathways in brick paviours that divides the garden into distinct planting areas encompassing herbs, flowers, fruits and vegetables.*

The Place to Start

Outside, even more than in, the "floor" has a huge impact on the overall effect, and decorating your garden has to start with the groundwork. Perversely, the smaller the area, the harder the "floor" has to work. Where there is plenty of space, sweeping lawns are fine. Where space is at a premium, it may hardly seem worth getting the mower out, and a combination of hard and soft "flooring" becomes both more sensible and visually pleasing. Just as inside, the basic choice comes down to hard and soft flooring – the hard being patios and paths, the soft being planting. But while a single surface running seamlessly from wall to wall looks wonderful inside, outside, in anything but the smallest patio, it is likely to look flat and dull. Introduce variation, texture and a change in levels to create a much more interesting vista.

If you can afford it, and you want to start from scratch, it really is worth getting the floor right, as that offers the best basic structure to the garden. Even the most charming planting, pots and decorative details are diminished when set against the tedium of uniform concrete slabs, while a well thought-out floor looks elegant even before the addition of a single plant. And in later years, it will be much easier to completely change the planting, pots, even the boundaries in order to create a new look, than to re-structure the ground.

Even if it really isn't feasible to go for major change, there are ways to improve the situation – perhaps by removing some of the slabs to increase the planting areas both around the perimeters and within the main paved areas. Or you could use decorative detailing to disguise parts of a less-than-pretty surface.

ABOVE: *Brick-shaped stone paviours set into a tiny lawn, then decorated with miniature urns mimic the vistas set out on the floors of classical gardens.*

LEFT: *The clay-tiled floor and brick retaining walls of an old greenhouse make an evocative home for a herb garden and a focal point within the whole context of this established English garden. The same effect could be achieved using any vitrified tiles designed for pathways, laid diagonally in alternating colours.*

OPPOSITE: *This tapestry of purple and lilac bordering herringbone-laid brick is reminiscent of a soft carpet on parquet flooring. Mosses, alpines and other low-growing plants have been allowed to take up residence on the curved York stone steps.*

Material Choices

Outdoors, little surpasses the beauty of natural stone, especially if it is a local stone which inherently harmonizes with its surroundings. Another good material you can use is brick, which again, if it is a local brick, will naturally blend with the house and garden. Only bricks with a flat surface are suitable for outside use, and even then, some are not frostproof. It is best to choose brick paviours, which are specially made for patios and paths. Aggregates are another kind of natural stone. These come in the form of gravel, which can be sharp but beds down well; or shingle, which has a similar appearance but, coming from the seaside, has more rounded grains. Other decorative, natural hard surfaces can be achieved with the clever use of pebbles, slate or ceramics. The not-so-hard-underfoot floorings come in wood, either as a custom-made timber decking or in the form of re-claimed materials, such as railway sleepers from disused tracks.

If natural hard flooring material is out of your price bracket, there is a wide choice of concrete paviours. Not all come in uniform, uninspired slabs: many have subtle variations in tone to give a naturally aged look and are available in varying sizes; some come in the form of ready-to-split blocks of cobbles, each of which comes away slightly differently, giving a more natural finished effect.

LEFT: *Stone paviours, laid end to end, visually elongate the path in the garden of this town terrace.*

LEFT: *Timber decking makes a delightful alternative to stone or concrete for patios or outdoor living areas. It can also solve problems in gardens which slope by providing a level raised platform from which to view the scene.*

When it comes to soft flooring, the most obvious solution is lawn. Planting also offers a soft floor, though this is usually a look-but-don't-walk area.

The choice of material is one thing, deciding on its best form for your garden is quite another. Stone, natural or otherwise, is available in slabs, rectangles, small squares, cobbles or crazy paving. Concrete also comes in any number of shapes, such as hexagons and octagons. The form you choose and the way in which the stones are laid can affect the whole look of the garden. Smaller units can make a tiny plot seem larger. Bricks laid widthways across a path can make it seem calmer; laid lengthways along the path, they lend dynamism. A herringbone arrangement is both attractive and lends a feeling of establishment, harking back to the Elizabethan era. Using different-sized units of the same material offers interesting variety, while diagonally laid rectangles can visually enlarge a tiny patio.

Changing the level in a garden immediately adds an extra dimension. Even a single step – perhaps up to a patio – gives the feeling of moving from one area to another, while lending visual depth to the whole garden. But beware: flights of more than two steps need plenty of space and can quickly eat into a small garden as each one needs to be at least 30cm (12in) deep. Flights of stairs leading down to the garden can be a real bonus, because it doesn't take much effort to make a feature of them. Pots of plants on each step always look charming, especially if they end in a flourish at the bottom with a carefully arranged group.

LEFT: *Miniature violas, one plant to a pot, make an enchanting decoration for old stone steps.*

LEFT: *A sweeping lawn makes an enviable natural emerald carpet, perfect for wetter climates.*

Floor Planting

Any kind of outdoor floor looks more established if small mosses, plants and lichens are allowed to take up residence between the paviours . . . though the finished effect can be greatly enhanced with a little judicious weeding. Self-seeded violas look enchanting; thistles aren't so appealing! On a slightly broader scale, you can cultivate mini-gardens or "lawns" by removing a paviour and planting in its place. This is a particularly effective way of softening uninspired areas of large concrete slabs. Try planting a miniature herb lawn that releases its aroma as you brush past. Chamomile (the non-flowering variety "Treneague") and thyme are particularly effective. Or you can plant with larger herbs, such as lavender or sage. Low-growing flowers, such as alyssum, violets, violas, pinks or any of the alpines, can offer a subtle but effective splash of floor-level colour.

ABOVE: *This fascinating three-dimensional, ceramic sun makes an original floor feature. Planted up with low-growing plants, such as mind-your-own-business, it takes on the appearance of a rich green tapestry that enhances the sun motif.*

LEFT: *A carpet of tiny alpine strawberries gives this floor an appealing summer look.*

ABOVE: *This floor has been given an extra dimension with an alpine garden planted into an old millstone.*

Alpine Wheel

There is something very appealing about alpines. The wonderful variety and texture of the plants are punctuated in the spring with the most delicate-looking flowers. They are not difficult to look after, and will eventually spread to create a rich tapestry. This wheel makes a refreshing change from the more popular rock garden. Make it as small or as large as you like, and calculate the number of plants needed by checking their spread on the plant label.

TOOLS AND MATERIALS

For a wheel about 250cm (8ft) in diameter:
2 × 15cm (6in) lengths of wood
String
Spade
Compost and fertilizer
Old drain cover
62 bricks
About 3 alpine plants with a 30cm (12in) spread, per section
Gravel to cover
Pebbles and slates for decoration

1 *Make a simple pair of compasses using the two pieces of wood linked by a piece of string the length of the radius of the wheel. Dig over the approximate area of the wheel and prepare the earth by adding compost and fertilizer. Using the compasses, mark out the circle, and place the drain cover in the centre. Place bricks around the circle to form "spokes".*

2 *Position the plants as desired. In this wheel, each section has been planted with a different variety, so that as they grow, they will help to define the design.*

3 *Sprinkle gravel between and around the plants, and finish the design with decorative pebbles and slates.*

Edgings

The way a path or a patio is edged plays an important part in the successful design of the flooring. Many of the well-designed concrete paviours and setts (small cobble-like paviours) have complementary kerb edgings. Another idea is to make edgings by laying paviours in a different direction to the rest of the path or patio or on their sides to provide a ridge; or use bricks set at an angle to create a zigzag edge. There are also specially designed edgings in stone, brick, concrete and metal. Alternatively, you can create your own in, say, shells or by making a border of corks "planted" upright at the edge of a bed. You could also create neat miniature hedging of, say, box or lavender.

LEFT: *Original Victorian rope edgings are enjoying renewed popularity, and many new ones are now available.*

RIGHT: *These antique, charcoal-coloured stone, undulated edgings would provide a neat finish to a town garden.*

BELOW: *Scallop shells left over from the dinner table or cajoled from the fishmonger make a delightful edging in soft coral shades that co-ordinate well with terracotta pavings.*

Making Patterns

There is a great tradition of elaborate "floors" for outside use. The Romans created intricate mosaics on courtyard floors, a skill that reached its zenith in richly decorated Islamic outdoor architecture. In the Middle East and India, decorative paths and walkways were composed of geometric patterns in ceramic tiles. Echoes of this style can be seen in Victorian English architecture where terraced houses have distinctive "tessellated" pathways, tiled in geometric patterns, usually forming squares, rectangles and triangles in black and white or cream, chocolate and terracotta.

Pebbles are another mosaic material with a centuries-old tradition. Their natural colours and smoothly rounded forms can be used to make exquisite textural panels or even complete garden floors. Again, simple geometric shapes are traditional, though in the hands of an artist given enough space, they can become elaborate, figurative works of art.

Floor patterns using plants have also been created through the ages. The most obvious examples of these are Elizabethan knot gardens and baroque parterres. An outline shape is formed using hedging in simple straight lines, geometric patterns or curves to create, in the case of a knot garden, an elaborate knot effect. Traditionally, different plants are then planted within each section of the knot. Parterres can be on a much grander scale, often incorporating topiary, lawns and highly formalized plantings.

LEFT: *A miniature parterre decorates the corner of a modern driveway.*

ABOVE: *Tessellated tiles rescued from a crumbling city pathway, destined for a builder's skip, make an enchanting detail in a flower bed.*

LEFT: *Even old hub caps from agricultural machinery can be used to add texture to an ordinary gravel pathway.*

Pretty Pebble Rug

Create an outdoor "fireside rug" from pebbles, broken garden pots and old china ginger-jar tops. The simple design is not difficult to achieve and makes an appealing, witty motif in a paved patio. However, a pebble panel like this will need to be laid at the same time as the rest of the paving. See the plan at the back of the book if you wish to follow this design in detail. This rug measures 60 × 91cm (2 × 3ft) and, although you could make one of any size, it would be easier to start off with a small one.

PREPARATION

First prepare the flat bed. If you are having your patio paved by contractors, you can ask them to do this, giving them the dimensions and position of the finished panel. The bed should be prepared to a depth of about 10cm (4in), allowing a 5cm (2in) clearance below the level of the rest of the paving. If you are doing the paving yourself, dig a pit 15cm (6in) deep and to the dimensions of the panel. Mix equal parts of fine aggregate and cement. Then, using a watering can, dribble in a little water at a time until you have a dry, crumbly mix. Use this to fill the area, leaving a 5cm (2in) clearance. Allow the mix to dry. Gather together plenty of materials for the design and lay them out for size on the dry bed before you begin. Using tile nippers, cut off the bottoms of at least six terracotta pots and snip off the rims in sections. Choose pebbles and slates that are long enough to bed in at least 2.5cm (1in) below the surface of the "rug".

AFTERCARE

Protect the rug for three days by covering it with a board raised on bricks then overlaid by plastic sheeting. Avoid walking on the rug for a month to allow the mortar to set.

TOOLS AND MATERIALS

Spade
Fine aggregate to fill the area to a depth of 10cm (4in)
Cement
Watering can
Water for mixing
Selection of pebbles, pieces of slate, terracotta pots, china-pot lid tops
Tile nippers
Sharp sand
Mortar colour
Straight edge
Hammer
Soft brush
Board to cover rug area
4 bricks
Plastic sheeting

1 *Prepare the mortar bedding by mixing equal quantities of sharp sand and cement. Add the mortar colour and mix in well. The design is worked while the mortar mix is dry, to enable you to change the design as you work. But the pebble rug has to be completed in a day because moisture from the atmosphere will begin to set the mortar.*

2 *Pour the dry mix onto the flat bed and, using a straight edge, smooth it out until it is level with the rest of the paving. Then remove a small quantity from the centre so the mix does not overflow as you work. This extracted mix can be re-added at a later stage, if necessary, as the design progresses.*

3 Starting from the outside and using the hammer, carefully tap in pebbles, slates and the rim sections from the terracotta pots to make a level, decorative border.

4 Brush the mortar over the worked areas to make sure any gaps are filled. To build up the border design, continue working towards the centre, carefully hammering in the pebbles, slates and terracotta as you go. Use the china pot lid tops to add a splash of colour to the four corners.

5 Work out a central design using the terracotta bases, pebbles and slate to provide a pleasing contrast with the border. Make sure the central area of mortar is flat, then, using the tile nippers, cut the pieces of terracotta rim to size as necessary. Gently hammer everything into position. When the pattern is complete, brush the mortar evenly over the finished surface. Finally, using a watering can with a fine sprinkler nozzle, dampen the surface. As the mortar absorbs the moisture, it will set hard.

Decorative Details

It pays dividends to give attention to ground detail as well as everywhere else in the garden room . . . and that doesn't mean just the hard paving areas. Flower beds, too, can be treated to a little accessorizing!

Any collection of flat objects can be used to add interest. Pebbles collected from the beach, old pieces of tile, glazed ceramics, shells or slates all look good when scattered on beds or in the tops of pots.

RIGHT: *Even artefacts as unprepossessing as old drain covers can look good when grouped together on the floor, creating a pleasing effect with their natural geometry.*

LEFT: *Pieces of old slate, buried end-on into concrete, make a wonderful textural floor plaque. In spring, young forget-me-nots can be planted round it to create a vibrant azure border.*

LEFT: *Highly glazed frostproof tiles, bricks and randomly shaped riven stone provide an unusual and decorative paving, reminiscent of a patchwork quilt.*

Miniature Pebble Circle

1 *Prepare a smooth circular area in the garden. Mark out the area for the finished circle using a makeshift pair of compasses (as described for the alpine wheel).*

2 *Add sufficient water to the sand and cement mix to achieve a crumbly consistency. Using a mortar trowel, smooth the cement into the circle.*

3 *Working quickly, before the cement sets, press in a border of slates.*

4 *Working in concentric rings, add a circle of old terracotta and another of slates, then a "wheel" of pebbles and terracotta.*

Here is a very simple mosaic made from pieces of slate and old terracotta plus a few beach pebbles, which can be used as a decorative detail anywhere in the garden.

TOOLS AND MATERIALS

5kg (11lb) bag of sand and cement mix

Mortar trowel

Slates, terracotta crocks and pebbles

WALLS AND WALL COVERINGS

It is the garden walls – and the decorations you put on them – that welcome visitors at eye level. So dress the walls well, using colour, texture, pictures and decorations.

OPPOSITE: *This ceramic tile panel makes the ideal outdoor picture, perfectly echoing its indoor cousin.*

Boundary Choices

Garden walls and fences are essentially functional. They are there to define the boundaries, to keep children and pets safely within and intruders out. Nevertheless, they also provide a design function, affording the garden its main vertical structure. Depending on the circumstances, this can be emphasized or played down. The obvious example for most houses is the contrast between the front and back gardens. At the front, fences are usually low or visually lightweight, creating a boundary without obscuring the house, to provide an open, welcoming look. At the back, however, the boundary walls are more likely to be solid to provide privacy from neighbouring gardens. They also form the background against which the garden can be planned. For this reason, the walls shouldn't be too dominant in themselves.

The most appealing garden walls have to be those of well-seasoned brick, evocative as they are of the walled gardens that are integral to large country homes. They lend an air of permanence, have a pleasing crumbly texture and, because they retain and reflect heat, they can create a protected micro-climate within the garden. Garden walls always look best built with local

OPPOSITE: *Clambering creamy-yellow roses make a summer decoration for a flint and brick wall, taking over from a memorable spring flowering of wisteria.*

BELOW: *Picket fencing makes for a simple yet efficient boundary. Leave it regimentally plain, or let climbers scramble over it, as here, for a softer look.*

materials – stone, flint or local stock brick. If you are building or repairing a wall, it is worth seeking out these local materials, even second-hand, as it will then blend in with its environment.

The most common garden "walls" consist of wooden lapped fencing, which is fortunately relatively inexpensive and easy to put up. It comes in panels, ready-treated against rot, and is nailed or screwed to posts fixed into a "collar" of long metal spikes, which have been firmly driven into the ground. A similarly solid-looking wall is wattle fencing. Woven from young willow branches, this traditional fencing dates back to the Bronze Age in Britain. Still with its bark intact, it provides a fine texture against which plants can grow and clamber. Wattle fencing is available as "hurdles" (panels) of various widths and heights, which can be erected as quickly and easily as the more commonplace wooden fencing.

Plants, too, can be used to create garden walls. Box and privet offer classic hedging that is nevertheless very appealing, providing a rich green boundary all year round. It can also be clipped into simple topiary

Above: *This living wall of roses makes a delightful garden boundary. Even grown over quite a flimsy frame of trelliswork or chain link, roses soon provide dense cover that protects privacy as much as any more solid planting.*

shapes, which look just as effective in small urban gardens as they do in larger rural ones. The trick is to keep them to the scale of the garden and its surroundings. Elaborate peacocks may look fantastic in the country; in urban situations, a neat orb or stately obelisk would be more appropriate.

Left: *This decorative trellis features panelling at its base, which has been painted in the same way as for an interior. This yellow-green shade always looks attractive with plants.*

Larger conifers, such as thuja, can also provide lofty verdant hedging, which is perfect for protecting your privacy in built-up areas. However, some conifers will eventually grow very tall – up to 15m (50ft) – so make sure you buy one of the more manageable varieties, such as Thuja "Lutea Nana", which stops at a modest height of about 183cm (6ft), or "Rheingold", which reaches 3–3.5m (10–12ft).

Another way of creating a living wall is to fix a trellis on which to grow climbers and ramblers. The classic choices are roses, honeysuckle, jasmine, clematis and potato vine (*Solanum jasminoides*), all of which produce flowers, for a fabulous floral wall. Cleverly planted, they can provide colour interest all year round. If your horticultural knowledge stops short of the encyclopaedic, plan the easy way, by buying a new climber in flower every two or three months. They will all come up again the following year, ensuring another lovely display of year-round colour.

LEFT: *Wattle fencing has been used in Europe for centuries. Made of woven willow, it provides a wonderful texture to the garden and improves with age as plants grow up and through it.*

Fences and Dividers

Privacy is not always the priority. At the front of the house, you may prefer to be a little more open and welcoming, while still needing a fence to define the boundary. These lighter "screens" could be low walls teamed with low hedging, such as the traditional box or privet, or a pretty floral hedge, such as lavender or fuchsia. Wood can make decorative front fencing, too. Traditional picket fencing looks wonderful in classic clean white or it can be painted to complement the plants. In country districts, rustic poles look good, especially if you don't want to obscure a wonderful view. They can be positioned either upright in lines or arranged in a series of long, low crosses to create a loose trellis. Metal is another perfect material for front fences. Railings, marching regimentally across the front garden, look smart in a city, while ornamental metal lattice or trellis looks decorative in all situations.

Another setting for lightweight or low fences is within the garden, to divide off areas such as those where special plantings have been made, or to define living areas or herb gardens.

LEFT: *Metal railings are the classic smart answer for front gardens in town, but they are just as pleasing when used to divide a rambling country plot. The appeal is the smart, almost military line they make that unequivocally says "no entry" without obstructing the view.*

LEFT: *White-painted picket fencing provides a classic boundary marker that is perennially pleasing. The crisp, uniform line of wooden posts, with its picot edging at the top, provides a framework to the garden that looks smart anywhere.*

ABOVE: *Crossed rustic poles bring charming restraint to unruly shrub roses*

LEFT: *Metal trelliswork, here decorated with charming cast metal flowers, makes the most delightful front-garden fencing.*

Entrances and Exits

Depending on where they are, garden gates and doors have different functions and different decorative appeal. Front gates welcome visitors, directing them towards the front door, and so, like front fences, are generally lower and more screen-like in appearance. Gates and doors at the side of the garden and leading into the back serve quite the opposite purpose, that of protecting against intruders, so they are generally more solid. They also play a very different visual role in the general design of the garden. They offer a break in the possible monotony of the wall and, since their presence suggests they lead somewhere, they can also lend an intriguing extra dimension to the garden. Even if it doesn't actually go anywhere, a door in a wall or fence gives the romantic impression of leading to a secret garden or another, unknown space. It also allows us a feeling of privacy: we, too, are in a secret place, accessible only to those we allow in.

OPPOSITE: *An exquisite, weathered wood and metal door makes a decorative garden entrance.*

ABOVE: *This tall, metal gate leads from one part of the garden to another, lending intrigue to a space that would have offered less interest had it been one large open area.*

ABOVE: *An ordinary, wooden-slat garden door leads from an alleyway to a tiny but enchanting city garden. The twig wreath gives just a hint of the delights to be found behind the door.*

Trelliswork

Trellis is a great garden material. It can be used as a wall in itself, providing a framework for climbers and ramblers. It can be used as a divider within the garden to lend perspective (which is dealt with in more detail in *Fixtures and Furniture*). It can be used to lend height to walls where extra privacy is needed and it can be used to decorate the walls themselves. The decorative aspect is especially valuable where the walls or fences are less than beautiful, or where you would like to add a little extra texture.

The trellis does not have to be ready-made. Old gates, an old window minus the panes, metal panels or panels made from vines and other organic materials all can serve the same purpose as ordinary trelliswork and have the advantage of looking good, even before the climbers have been planted. More traditional trellis-work can also be given a head start with a lick of paint, which immediately gives it a more finished and individual appearance.

ABOVE: *Here, painted square trellis has been used as a screen, dividing off one part of the garden. It provides an excellent framework for a climbing rose and clematis. This trellis can also be a pretty solution for a boundary wall.*

RIGHT: *An old wrought-iron gate provides an elegant trellis framework for a miniature rose.*

ABOVE: *A fabulous, Indian metal trellis panel makes an imaginative framework for a special feature. The frame has been painted in verdigris colours and duck-egg blue urns, planted with saxifrage, complete the picture.*

RIGHT: *Evocative, organic twig trellis panels make a wonderful framework for a montage of climbing roses and additional decorative features such as twiggy hearts and stars and metal lanterns.*

Adding Colour

Inside the house, once the walls are plastered, you would immediately want to decorate them. Outside, people are still a little frightened of colour, preferring to play safe by sticking to the natural tones of stone, brick and wood. Nobody would dream of painting a beautiful old stone or brick wall anyway. But if your new fencing is the popular panelled variety, it is likely to arrive coated in a preservative to protect it from rot, which usually comes in a violent shade of rust that you will probably want to cover up fast. In a decorative garden room, colour is very important. Not only can the paint you choose suggest mood and ambience, just as it does inside, it can also be used to emphasize the colour scheme of the garden planting.

The surfaces you paint may be the house walls, walls of outside buildings or the garden walls. Maybe you have a hotchpotch of fencing and trelliswork, all of slightly different woods and ages, that has resulted in a visual muddle. Paint them all in the same decorative finish and you will have a much more coherent look. Or you may have newly erected trelliswork that has a year or more to wait for a verdant covering of creepers. Paint it and you will have a reasonable finish while the plants grow.

ABOVE: *Sugar-almond shades differentiate the two properties. In the far garden, the pastel pink perfectly matches the climbing rose behind.*

LEFT: *It is easy to create a strong impact by using the same shade on wall and furniture. Here, the trelliswork and bench have been painted to match, creating a finished look even before the plants have become established.*

Colour can also be used to highlight areas. You may pinpoint an area destined for a particular colour scheme or you may wish to highlight the planting. Burnt-orange fencing would provide a stunning background for marigolds, while yellow picket would highlight the nodding heads of yellow pansies.

Painted fences and surfaces also lend colour throughout the year. They are particularly valuable in

LEFT: *A decorative edge in stripes of bright Caribbean colours gives life to a plain white wall and door. Masking tape was used to keep the lines straight and, when they were all complete and dry, the leaves were stencilled in position.*

BELOW: *The texture of the brickwork lends depth to any colour you add.*

winter when many plants have died down. This is the ideal time to paint them with a fresh coat, perhaps bearing in mind the colours of the blooms that will come up in spring. It is not difficult to quickly add colour as, unlike inside, you don't need a lot of time for preparation when the subject of your attention is rough-sawn wood. There is no need to fill holes or sand down. Just give the wood a good scrub to clean it – and allow it to dry thoroughly – before applying the colour. If you plan to paint a house wall, however, you will obviously need to prepare the surface thoroughly before applying the colour.

Ideas with Paint

Whether you want to paint your garden wall or a house wall that makes up part of the garden, there is plenty of inspiration to be had. Experiment not only with colour but with technique. As well as straight colour, you can create depth by layering the colours. Try *trompe l'oeil* effects such as marble, stone, slate or moss. Stencil onto walls, use potato prints, geometric designs or even add simple motifs. The trick is to consider the scale. These effects will have to be seen from much further away than they would be if used inside the house. Even a 9m (30ft) garden is a good deal larger than the average room, so everything has to be exaggerated a little. Paint effects need to be a little less subtle; motifs, generally larger.

ABOVE: *A chequerboard pattern always makes a striking display and is a traditional design in many communities, so it is unlikely to date. This one in tan and cream was inspired by African decoration; the same design in china-blue and white would evoke Provence. A chequerboard is easy to paint. Like this one, it doesn't necessarily have to be neat and even; little irregularities simply add to its charm. If you trust your eye, paint it freehand, using a fine brush to create the outline of each square and then filling it in later with a wider brush if the squares are large. If you fancy something a little more orderly, cut a large square stencil and position it on the wall. Chequerboard a whole wall if you are feeling adventurous or simply work it on window and door reveals and along skirting areas.*

ABOVE: *This cascade of falling leaves was created using a potato print, which can be just as effective outside as in. Choose a simple motif, like this oak leaf, and, using the point of a knife, gently "draw" the outline onto the cut surface of half a large potato. Cut away the potato from around the outline to a depth of about 8mm (¼in) and "draw" in the veins. Give the wall a pale colourwash base. When that has fully dried, dip the potato into a stronger colour of paint, stamp it onto a piece of newspaper to remove the excess, then stamp onto the wall.*

ABOVE: *Marbling makes the perfect effect for an outside wall, since it works best in oil-based paints that are ideal for outside use. It should be applied to a smooth surface. The veins are applied over a paint base while it is still wet and further splashes of white spirit are added to soften the hard edges.*

ABOVE: *Evocative of the sunny Mediterranean, lemons and limes make wonderful motifs that anyone can manage. Use the template at the back of the book if you wish. Paint the shapes randomly like this or make a* trompe l'oeil *by painting a simple shelf of plates decorated with lemons.*

ABOVE: *An unprepossessing garden or shed wall gives the impression of having the patina of time when stippled in shades of green and yellow to give a mossed effect. First apply a colourwash of a mid to dark green, then roll on a pale green and, finally, stipple on some ochre by holding the brush vertically to dab on the paint.*

ABOVE: *Naive lizard-like animal motifs are traditional in many communities. This one, inspired by African art, is not dissimilar to motifs used by American Indians. Perhaps its appeal is partly due to the fact that it is rooted deep in our common subconscious, or perhaps its charm is in its simplicity. Just one lizard in the corner of a sunny wall would transform it from the ordinary to something special. Use the template at the back of the book if you wish.*

Decorating a Shed

Even the most unpromising garden buildings can be turned into something special. When this one was "inherited" with the garden, it was little more than a concrete block. With the addition of some plaster shapes and paint, it took on the appearance of a miniature Mediterranean villa.

TOOLS AND MATERIALS

Pencil
Stiff paper
Scissors
MDF (medium-density fibreboard)
Jigsaw or fretsaw
Acrylic wood primer
Decorating brush
Dark blue emulsion paint
Fine-textured masonry paint in white
Acrylic scumble glaze
Water for mixing
Artist's acrylic paint in light blue, red, orange and yellow
Soft cloths
Nails
Hammer
Stiff brush
Exterior tile adhesive
Selection of small, decorative plaster shapes from architectural plaster suppliers
Electrical tape
Panel pins
Natural sponge
Artist's brush
Polyurethane varnish
Decorating brush for varnish

1 *Draw a Moresque roof motif on the piece of paper to fit the top of the door. Check the size against the door. Cut out and place this template on the MDF, drawing around its shape. Cut out using a jigsaw or fretsaw.*

2 *Paint both the door and the MDF shape with acrylic wood primer and allow to dry for one to two hours. Paint one coat of dark blue emulsion and allow to dry for two to three hours.*

3 *Mix up a glaze using fine-textured masonry paint, acrylic scumble glaze and a little water to the consistency of double cream, then tint with light blue acrylic artist's colour. Paint this onto the door and roof shape in the direction of the grain.*

4 *Quickly wipe off the glaze with a soft cloth to knock back the colour. Nail the MDF shape to the top of the door, and paint the nail heads with the pale blue glaze.*

5 Using a stiff brush, scrub the wall surfaces to remove the dirt. "Butter" exterior tile adhesive onto the surface of each decorative plaster shape. Fix them to the wall. Use electrical tape and panel pins to hold them in position while the adhesive dries overnight.

6 Remove the tape and pins, then paint the wall with one coat of fine-textured masonry paint and leave to dry for four to six hours.

7 Tint three pots of acrylic scumble glaze with acrylic paint – one red, one orange, one yellow – to the consistency of single cream. Using a damp sponge, wipe the colours randomly onto the wall, blending the edges. Wipe off the excess with a cloth.

8 Using an artist's brush, stipple extra colour into any detailing to add emphasis. Leave to dry for at least four hours. Once it is thoroughly dry, varnish the wall.

Colour-theme Plantings

Create impact in the garden by colour-theming seasonal planting with the walls. This works best with plants in containers as the containers can be chosen or painted to tone with the walls, then planted with flowers in complementary colours. Once the blooms are over, they can be replaced by new plantings for the next season. You don't have to always match the colours; you may decide to use complementary or even contrasting colours instead. In this way, the garden looks fresh and bright all year round and you have several scene changes as the seasons pass.

LEFT: *The bluey green and purple tones of ornamental cabbages look fabulous in an old galvanized bucket against the blue-green background of a painted fence.*

BELOW: *Fences stained in softer, bluey grey-greens set off all manner of greenery, including the foliage of this hebe. The pot has been painted in stripes to link the greens with the pink blooms.*

ABOVE: *Blues and greys make a wonderful combination and even the most rudimentary of garden paraphernalia can be put to good decorative use. This old, blue-painted wheelbarrow, set against a blue wall, creates impact, while making an original container for delicate blue violas.*

LEFT: *A yellow poppy and yellow violas look stunning planted up in golden pots, set against the warm ochre shades of a brick wall.*

Adding the Decorations

Once you are happy with the colour of the walls, you can start to add a more personal touch with the decorations. The most obvious garden decorations are wall-hung pots, sconces, brackets and small items of statuary. But almost any weatherproof collection could find a home on the garden wall. Birdcages, birdfeeders, shells, lanterns and willow or wire wreaths can be suspended on a wall. Or make a feature of wall-mounted shelves by filling them with pots, bottles, baskets, enamel or galvanized ware.

LEFT: *A cast-iron wall sconce makes a charming container for miniature marguerites, peeping shyly through the more exuberant clambering golden roses.*

OPPOSITE: *This beautiful stone wall bracket makes the perfect garden "statuary" for a tiny patio.*

BELOW: *A group of galvanized containers makes a shapely collection on a cottage wall, their wonderful, soft metal shades blending harmoniously with the garden.*

Stone-effect Wall Mask

This wonderful stone-effect wall mask, evocative of medieval times, unbelievably started off as terracotta-coloured plastic. The slightly pitted quality of the plastic makes it very suitable for painting and once the mask is in position on the garden wall, surrounded by climbers, nobody will suspect that it is not made from natural stone.

TOOLS AND MATERIALS

Plastic wall mask
Medium-grade sandpaper
Acrylic primer
Decorating brush
Stone-coloured emulsion paint
Acrylic scumble glaze
Artist's acrylic paint in raw umber, white, yellow ochre and burnt umber
Water for thinning
Natural sponge
Large artist's brush
Matt Teflon-based polyurethane varnish
Decorating brush for varnish

1 *Sand the wall mask and paint it with acrylic primer. Allow to dry for one to two hours. Paint with one coat of stone-coloured emulsion. Allow to dry for two hours.*

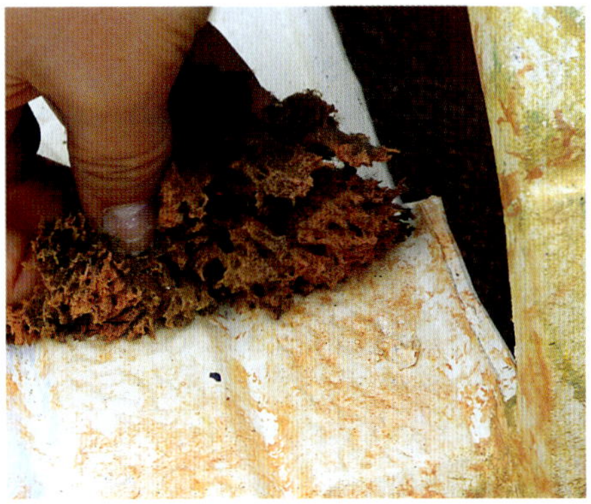

2 *Tint some of the acrylic scumble glaze with a little raw umber and thin with a little water. Sponge onto the mask. Allow to dry for one to two hours.*

3 *Tint some white acrylic paint with a little yellow ochre. Add to some scumble glaze and sponge on. Allow to dry for one to two hours.*

4 *Tint some more white acrylic paint with burnt umber and thin with a little water. Load the artist's brush and spatter onto the mask in flicking movements. Allow to dry and varnish.*

Pictures

Few walls inside the house are complete until the pictures are hung and there is no reason why pictures should not be hung outside, too. They obviously need to be weatherproof, however, so the conventional indoor types would not be suitable. Ceramic tiled panels, mosaics, old enamel advertisements or painted wood panels make excellent outdoor pictures.

RIGHT: *A quirky, ceramic, mosaic face sculpture smiles out through a "wall" of ivy.*

BELOW: *A pair of ceramic tile plaques echo the colour of the painted arbours and furniture.*

SOFT FURNISHINGS

The garden's soft furnishings are its plants, so use them to special effect when decorating your outdoor room. Let them soften windows like curtains and create focal points of colour like upholstery.

OPPOSITE: *Verdant greenery drapes luxuriously around this window in a living curtain that echoes the most elaborate indoor window treatment.*

Decorative Planting

Once the basic framework of the garden is in place, the fun can start with the soft furnishing. Inside, you would be thinking of comfortable furniture, curtains and carpet. Outside, it is the planting that provides the soft furnishing. Without it, the garden would look very rigid and uninviting. Add a few plants and immediately it takes on a much more comfortable feel. This is the part of gardening that can be the most absorbing, even if you have no horticultural knowledge. A trip to the garden centre to browse among the seasonal plants becomes a treat.

Putting together colours and textures to add to the border is where your own creativity comes in. But soft furnishing in our context is not just about borders, it is about all of the decorative planting that transforms an ordinary garden into a decorative garden room. It is about the climbers that clamber curtain-like over arches and soften the outlines of windows, and the hanging baskets that decorate walls. It is about the low-growing plants that create carpets of colour over what may previously have been uninspired floors. It is also about the plants that grow around and through old furniture in wilder gardens, creating a softness that hints at greater comfort. It is finally about the feature planting in containers, positioned at focal points of the garden to create added interest or greater impact.

ABOVE: *The face of a cherub, in reflective mood, peers through the ivy, adding a charming touch to the eaves of a garden shed.*

LEFT: *Statuesque Greek pithoi are used here for architectural interest, rather than for planting. However, they have been softened and beautifully set off by stately euphorbias in vibrant lime-greens.*

OPPOSITE: *A floral arbour makes a rich decorative frame for a piece of statuary, creating a theatrical effect. The roses, foxgloves and clematis make perfect stage curtains for this pensive stone player.*

Plants and Containers

The best way to create impact with seasonal flowers is to contain them in pots or some kind of container, as that way you can mass colour in the plantings and group or stack the pots for an even greater show. Containers are fabulous in any garden – first, because the vessel itself, however simple, gives architectural form; second, because it allows you to put the plants and colour exactly where you want them. You need a little colour high up? Plant up a plant stand, hanging basket or wall-mounted container. You need a little extra colour in a flower bed? Add a pot of colour, setting it down among the greenery. You can even plant up small pots to nestle on the top soil of larger ones for a rich, stacked effect.

ABOVE: *White violas in old terracotta pots, white-crusted with age, lend an ethereal air to the white-painted windowsill of the conservatory.*

LEFT: *Ornate Chinese ceramic pots make a delightful decorative feature when planted with toning flowering plants such as geraniums and petunias and accessorized with complementary Chinese statues.*

Little matches the earthiness of ordinary clay pots. They blend happily with their surroundings and complement the plants. Make sure they are frostproof if they are to serve when temperatures plummet, otherwise you will find the terracotta flaking off at the rim in the winter months.

Clay pots look different, depending on where they are from. Pots that are traditional in northern European countries, reminiscent of Beatrix Potter stories, are generally very red in hue, but the colour does soften with age as salts naturally form on the surface. You can hasten this look by scrubbing them with garden lime. Just make up a thick paste by adding a little

ABOVE: *For a gloriously rich, banked window display, one window box has been fixed to the front edge of the windowsill, while the other sits on the ledge. The planting scheme of petunias and dianthus in pinks and purples creates a greater impact for being colour co-ordinated and is complemented by the glorious lilac orbs of the alliums in the foreground.*

RIGHT: *Charming cast-iron panels are used here to enclose ordinary plastic pots of plants – a lovely idea that makes seasonal changes easy.*

water to the lime, then brush it on with an old washing-up brush. As the water in the lime dries out, the terracotta will acquire a soft, white bloom. Garden lime is excellent as it is not harmful to the garden (in fact, it is used as a fertilizer) and it won't inhibit the natural mould growth that also enhances the patina of age. Pots can also be aged by rubbing them with natural yoghurt then leaving them in a damp, shady place to encourage mould growth, but this takes longer.

Clay pots from the Mediterranean look very different to those from northern Europe. Greek pithoi, for example, traditionally used to store grain and oil, come in many elegant shapes and a wonderful sandy colour. Some are even frostproof.

Your choice does not have to be restricted to garden pots. Any container will do, as long as drainage holes can be drilled in the base. Try using old beer barrel halves, decorative ceramic pots (many are now being imported from the Far East), old chimney pots, buckets, agricultural baskets, such as potato pickers, or traditional garden baskets, such as wooden trugs. With a little imagination, shopping baskets, birdcages and lanterns can become hanging baskets; old olive oil cans in a row can become window boxes.

ABOVE: *All kinds of things can be used to add height to planting – particularly useful in spring and early summer when plants are still low. Here, a metal, stacking pan storage tower makes for brilliant high-level planting.*

ABOVE: *Even a couple of ordinary terracotta garden pots hanging on the wall make interesting decorative detail, especially when they are both planted with a froth of white blooms.*

Decorating and Planting a Window Box

Window boxes provide a delightful finish to windows, almost bringing the garden into the house. Being flat-fronted, they are also easier to decorate than rounded pots. Here, mussel shells lend impact to a co-ordinated planting of lavender and violas. Experiment with different shapes, using some mussel shells face up and others face down.

TOOLS AND MATERIALS

Small terracotta window box
Mussel shells
Glue gun and hot-wax glue sticks
Crocks or pebbles
Compost
Trowel
Water-retaining granules
Fertilizer granules
2 lavender plants
Tray of young viola plants
Watering can

1 When you are satisfied with your design, fix the shells in position on the window box, using a glue gun and hot-wax glue sticks.

2 Place crocks or pebbles over the drainage holes inside the window box.

3 Partly fill the box with compost, adding water-retaining and fertilizer granules as you go.

4 *Place the lavender at the back of the box. Press extra compost in front of them until it is the right height for the violas. Plant the violas on this "raised bed".*

5 *Press more compost firmly around all the plants and water generously.*

Hanging Gardens

When you want colour high up or relating to the building, the easiest way is to create a hanging garden, either in a basket or in a wall-mounted container. Ready-made hanging baskets are designed so that as the flowers grow, they cascade through the side struts and spill over the edge in a joyous show of colour, soon covering the whole basket. An alternative is to make the basket or container part of the display. Ordinary shopping baskets, buckets, agricultural containers, even kitchen equipment, such as colanders, pots and pans, can all be used as hanging baskets.

If the containers are large and possibly too heavy to be supported, one trick is to put a layer of broken up expanded polystyrene (from plant trays or electrical goods packaging) in the bottom of the container. This is lighter than the equivalent amount of compost and provides good drainage. Containers should have drainage holes and baskets will need lining to stop the soil from being washed out while you are watering. Liners can be home-made from a piece of plastic cut to size, with a layer of moss tucked between the basket and plastic for a more decorative look. Alternatively, you can use a proprietary liner, made from paper pulp, to fit purpose-made hanging baskets, or coconut matting – which comes in a variety of shapes and sizes to adapt to all kinds of baskets.

Whatever type of container you choose, it needs to be filled with a good compost, and adding fertilizer granules and water-retaining granules can also help promote luscious results.

ABOVE: *The most unlikely items can be used as hanging baskets. This pretty metal lantern from the Middle East has been filled with terracotta pots planted with variegated ivies, to make a surprising and decorative hanging feature.*

ABOVE: *Wall-mounted, miniature mangers stacked one over the other make a vibrant column of colour in a tiny courtyard garden.*

ABOVE: *A witty interpretation of a hanging basket, this Indian birdcage makes an ideal receptacle for potted plants. Hung in a mulberry tree, it lends floral interest in early spring before the leaves have burst.*

Planting up a Summer Basket

Hanging baskets are summer favourites in even the smallest of gardens, bringing a floral splash – and fragrance if you choose appropriate plants – to walls, verandas, patios and even basement areas. Plant them early in the year, once the threat of late frosts has passed, to give them time to "get their toes in" and fill out.

TOOLS AND MATERIALS

Hanging basket with chains or rope
Coconut liner
Compost
Trowel
Water-retaining granules
Fertilizer granules
6 variegated ivies
Bucket of water
2 diascia
6 verbenas
Watering can

1 *Line the basket with coconut liner and part fill with compost, adding water-retaining granules and fertilizer granules as you go, according to the manufacturers' instructions.*

2 *Separate out the ivy plants, then thread them through the sides of the basket. Place a diascia plant at either end of the basket. Add the verbenas.*

3 *Press more compost around each plant and down the sides of the basket so that they are all firmly bedded in. Water generously and hang the basket.*

Colour Splash Plantings

Just as you can decorate the inside of the home with colourful flower arrangements, so you can outside. Use pots of flowering plants to provide a colourful splash in a prominent part of the garden or to decorate the outdoor living area when entertaining. Create an immediate colour impact by choosing a colour theme and teaming containers and plants in toning shades. Try painting some terracotta pots specially to match your favourite flowers. You could also make a tablescape for a special occasion, using a variety of containers and seasonal flowering plants in perhaps hot clashing colours or in cool shades of blue, purple and white.

ABOVE: *Create a colour splash for summer parties. Here, hot colours vie and clash in a fabulous, vibrant display. Simple enamel tableware and a wire "coffee pot" make witty containers for strawberry plants, geraniums, verbenas in magenta and scarlet, pansies and daisy-like, yellow creeping zinnia.*

ABOVE: *White-painted pots planted with lily of the valley and placed on a stone bracket, make a supremely elegant springtime feature.*

ABOVE RIGHT: *A selection of auriculas planted in an old stone urn and overhung with berberis make a rich spring planting in shades of burnished copper, reminiscent of an old sepia photograph.*

RIGHT: *The blue-green leaves of the pinks and oxalis perfectly complement the rich verdigris patina on this old, copper builder's bucket from France, creating a striking feature that can be hung in the garden or near the house. It's a brilliant way to bring colour up to eye level in spring, when the plants are still low.*

Creating Cameo Gardens

It is delightful to plan cameo gardens within gardens. They can provide a surprise in a small corner, embellish a less-than-full area or even provide a miniature project for children who would love to have an area of their own. The idea is to find a theme – herbs, perhaps, or pansies, miniature vegetables or lavender – then make up a "sampler", providing a different container for èach variety. Alternatively, you can make the containers the theme, choosing watering cans, culinary pots, pans and colanders, enamelware or terracotta in different shapes and sizes. Another idea is to design a miniature formal garden, perhaps taking inspiration from the classic Italian style. Choose a piece of miniature statuary as a focal point, then clip some young box plants into a miniature hedge surround and fill in with a dwarf lavender.

LEFT: *An old lead sink becomes home to a decorative miniature vegetable garden. Two varieties of lettuce and one of mint – restrained from over-exuberant growth by being planted within its own concealed pot – provide a pleasing textural variety.*

LEFT: *Thyme gardens have a history that goes back through the centuries. Their appeal is the irresistible aroma combined with the almost endless number of varieties, with leaves that range in shape from round to needle-like; in texture from smooth to woolly; in colour from silver to darkest green. The trick is to choose a selection to create a rich tapestry. Planting them up in small terracotta pots keeps the garden to a scale in which the miniature size of the leaves and their various textures can be appreciated.*

RIGHT: *This terracotta garden is focused around tall, long-tom pots planted with hostas, ivies and clematis left loose so that it behaves like a trailer, rather than a climber. Old drain covers and edging tiles add richness.*

BELOW: *Serried ranks of watering cans in the soft greys of weathered, galvanized metal make a beautiful feature in themselves. Planted up with hostas and violas, they become a highly original cameo garden.*

Tin-can Plant Nursery

Seedlings can be decorative in themselves, so prick them out from their seed trays into a collection of aluminium cans mounted onto a plaque. They can grow there, high above any threatening late frosts, until they are ready to be planted out. The plaque itself looks wonderful made from ordinary aluminium cans, but if you want to add a bit more colour, scour the continental delicatessens and enjoy some culinary treats at the same time.

TOOLS AND MATERIALS

Piece of board, about 60 × 30cm (24 × 12in)
Undercoat
Coloured gloss paint
Decorating brush
Can opener
Variety of empty aluminium cans with the labels removed
Metal snippers
Pliers
Nail
Hammer
Box of tin tacks

1 *Apply an undercoat followed by a coat of gloss paint to the board, allowing each coat to dry completely.*

2 *Use the can opener to remove the top of each can if this has not already been done. Wash out the cans thoroughly.*

3 *Using metal snippers, cut down the side of each can and cut off half of the bottom.*

4 *Open out the sides with pliers and snip a V-shape into each one. Pierce the bottom of each can, using a nail and hammer.*

5 *Try out the arrangement of the cans on the board. Then, using one tin tack at each side point of the cans, nail into position.*

Dea
Dea
Dea
White Tower
ΟΜΟΣΠΟΝΔΙΑΣ
OMOSPONDIAS
THESSALONIKI
GREECE - GRIECHENLAND

Witty Ways with Everyday Plants

Interesting gardens don't have to depend on a horticulturalist's knowledge of plants. Even the most ordinary plants can take on an exotic personality if pruned or planted in an original way. Many garden centres now sell ready-trained or standardized shrubs – you can add your own touch with a witty container, pretty underplanting or an attractive way of tying them up.

Topiary has come back into fashion, but this time it isn't restricted to large, formal gardens tended by teams of gardeners. Box and privet grown in pots can be kept to a manageable size and still be clipped into architectural globes and conical shapes.

LEFT: *As a change from allowing roses to scramble up walls or trellises, this one has been trained around a simple obelisk, the diagonally trailing stems adding greatly to its decorative appeal.*

LEFT: *Small-scale topiary can be arranged, as here, in groups or used as boundary markers, down the edges of paths, between beds or to section off different parts of the garden.*

LEFT: *A standardized hydrangea grown in a pot makes an excellent patio plant. It has the appealing appearance of a miniature tree and you can enjoy its flamboyant blooms without any worry that it might take over the garden.*

LEFT: *Small gardens don't have to preclude the inclusion of fruit trees. Here, a decorative, trained apple is flanked by pillars of ballerina crab apples which grow in a pole-like fashion. The raffia heart has been tied on as decoration.*

FIXTURES AND FURNITURE

Fixtures such as sheds, arches, screens and shelving are the elements that begin to lend structure to the garden. Add a few well-chosen items of furniture, and the outdoor living is easy.

OPPOSITE: *A gracious walkway of fruit trees trained over arches leads to a water feature bordered by orbs of clipped box.*

Dividers and Arches

Even the smallest garden can accommodate fixtures such as arches, arbours, pergolas, trellis divides or a small garden shed or play house. And while the hard landscaping and the herbaceous borders dictate the layout of the garden, it is these vertical elements that greatly affect its structure and overall look. Vertical structures such as pergolas and garden buildings can be positioned around the garden's perimeter, while rose arches, walkways and trellis screens can be used as dividers. Anything that divides the garden lends extra perspective because it defines another space and, even in gardens that are fairly limited in size, being able to glimpse beyond into another area creates the illusion of greater space.

If you want to screen off part of the garden – to create an eating area perhaps or to section off a vegetable garden – the simplest solution is to use trellis. Trellis is wonderfully versatile and comes in a variety of panel shapes and sizes. As well as the basic rectangular panels, there are panels with pointed, convex or concave tops and even with integral "windows", all of which provide plenty of scope for creativity. When it comes to finishing touches, there is a wide choice of attractive finials in shapes such as globes, acorns, pineapples and obelisks.

You don't have to screen off a whole area to lend perspective. Even a rose arch spanning the garden path can have the desired effect. Either buy a ready-made metal arch or make a simple wooden one using pergola poles or posts with short rafters or crossbeams across the top. Another way of making an arch is to use the plants themselves, planting young trees either side of a path, for example, then tying them together at the top so they grow into an arch.

Above: *Trellis screens can divide off part of the garden to create the illusion of space or to emphasize a focal point – in this case, a water feature. Trellis panels come in a wide variety of sizes and shapes, and the supporting posts can be finished off with architectural finials such as globes or obelisks. The screen can then be painted for a decorative finish.*

Above: *Here, a couple of young firs have been trained onto a metal frame to create what will eventually be a surprisingly substantial archway over this gravel path.*

LEFT: *Roses scrambling over an archway are a quintessential ingredient of a country garden. As well as bringing a delightful froth of blooms high above their natural position, the archway creates a simple screening effect that offers an illusion of space.*

Walkways, Pergolas and Arbours

As well as serving as a light screen, arches can mark the beginning of a walkway. If you have sufficient space in the garden, a walkway has great appeal. There is something peaceful and cloister-like about a walkway beneath a leafy tunnel through which natural light filters to the ground. Even in a small garden, a simple, verdant archway offers a sense of romantic adventure – the idea of going somewhere.

Walkways can be as simple as an elongated archway – probably the best option in small gardens – or a long snaking affair down one side of the garden. They can be made from metal or from wooden poles in a series of archways. The effect of a walkway can be made even more powerful if punctuated at the end by a focal point, classical style. In a formal garden, this may all have been planned as part of the landscaping, the walkway leading perhaps to a door or gateway or an exquisite piece of garden statuary. But you can adapt the idea for a more modest setting and create impact. A specimen plant or a favourite pot or container beautifully planted up will provide a satisfying focal point at the end of the walkway, while acquiring a greater sense of importance for itself as it attracts the attention of everyone who saunters there.

Pergolas are first cousins to walkways, being covered areas usually fixed onto one side of the house. These work well in all sizes of garden, providing an attractive, natural, covered outdoor "room" and serving as a transition area between the inside and out. They make delightful shady outdoor eating areas that afford extra privacy from overlooking flats or close neighbours in, say, terraced streets.

Leafy arbours can lend architectural form to a garden while taking up very little space. Tucked against a wall, an arbour can create structure in even the smallest garden, offering somewhere shady to sit, relax and perhaps read or chat with a friend. At its simplest, an arbour could be formed by training climbing plants up a wall to form an arch over a garden bench, though it is not difficult to make a more permanent structure.

LEFT: *Flanked by greenery and shaded overhead by a roof of honeysuckle, this delightful arbour is set against the fabulous texture of a brick and flint wall. By incorporating the existing structure of the garden, it takes on an authentic "lived-in" feel. The weathered, rustic wooden bench and table are left out throughout the year, offering further structure to that part of the garden.*

ABOVE: *Cascades of laburnum make a flamboyant golden walkway.*

ABOVE: *This pagoda-topped metal walkway lends an almost oriental feel to the garden. Beautiful old Greek pithoi set in a bed of vibrant euphorbia and hellebores are used to great effect as the focal point at the end.*

RIGHT: *A simple timber framework forms the "bones" of this pergola, but once the climbers have grown over the structure it is transformed into a lavish outdoor living area, decorated with a natural verdant wall covering.*

Trellis Arbour

An arbour is one of the easiest ways to introduce architectural structure to even the smallest of gardens . . . and it is no more difficult to make one than it is to put up a fence. This arbour is made up of trellis panels, then painted with a decorative outdoor stain to tone with the bench. The result is an enchanting, original bower.

TOOLS AND MATERIALS

Lattice (diagonal) trellis in the following panels:
- *3 panels 183 × 60cm (6 × 2ft)*
- *2 panels 183 × 30cm (6 × 1ft)*
- *1 concave panel 183 × 46cm (6 × 1½ft)*
- *1 panel 183 × 91cm (6 × 3ft)*

6 timber posts 7.5 × 7.5cm (3 × 3in), each 2.2m (7ft) long
Saw
6 spiked metal post supports 7.5 × 7.5cm (3 × 3in), each 76cm (2½ft) long
Mallet
10 × 5cm (2in) galvanized nails
Hammer
Electric drill with No.8 bit, and screwdriver attachment
40 × 3cm (1¼in) No.10 zinc-coated steel screws
2.5 litre (½ gallon) can exterior woodstain
Small decorating brush

1 *Gather together the trellis panels and "dry assemble" to ensure you are happy with the design. Two of the 183 × 60cm (6 × 2ft) panels are for the sides and the third is for the top. The two narrow panels and the concave panel are for the front and the 183 × 91cm (6 × 3ft) panel is to be used horizontally at the top of the back. Trim the wooden posts to length. They should be 183cm (6ft) plus the depth of the metal "shoe" at the top of the metal spike which will hold the post.*

2 *Start with the back panel. The posts need to be placed 183cm (6ft) apart. Mark their positions, then, using a mallet, drive in a spiked metal post. Drive a ready-trimmed post into each of the metal "shoes". Using the galvanized nails and the hammer, temporarily fix the top of the trellis to the top of the posts. Using a No.8 bit, drill holes for the screws at intervals down each side of the trellis. Screw in the screws.*

3 *In the same way, position the front outside posts and fix the side panels, then the inside front posts and front panels. Fix the concave panel into the panels either side of it. Finally, fix the roof in position, screwing it into the posts. Paint the arbour with exterior decorative woodstain and leave to dry.*

Garden Buildings

Any kind of garden building adds to the outdoor architecture and there are few gardens that don't have one, be it a garden shed, summer house, play house, folly or gazebo. They are usually left just as they were when they were put up, but it is never too late to turn them into decorative features in their own right. Garden sheds can be decorated, perhaps in stripes, like a beach hut, or given a more substantial-looking roof of slates. Climbers can be grown up them or pots grouped around them. Play houses, too, can be decorated to give them fairy-tale appeal. Honeysuckle or clematis could be grown over the roof and hanging baskets hung under the eaves.

Follies were a favourite in the gardens of Victorian homes, as were ornamental Japanese or oriental gardens. It is not difficult to incorporate some fun in the form of a folly – a Gothic shed, pagoda or temple. These can be bought ready to put up, or you could scour architectural salvage yards for attractive doors and windows that can be assembled into a new design.

ABOVE: *Architectural salvage, some pillars and posts, plenty of imagination plus a lick of paint make an eyecatching latter-day garden folly.*

LEFT: *A traditional gazebo, complete with pagoda roof, makes a charming outdoor seating area while adding architectural interest to a small garden.*

LEFT: *This delightful gazebo is simply made from a metal frame overgrown with climbers.*

Customized Play House

You can create an enchanting fairy-tale house that will add interest to the garden, while providing a play area the children will love. Give yourself a head start by buying one off the shelf and customizing it. Play houses usually come pre-treated for rot, which means they already have an excellent base for decoration (but do check this before you buy). This one has been given a slate roof with terracotta baby ridge tiles, shutters and a decorative fascia and, finally, a coat or two of paint. This represents quite a few skills, so you could restrict yourself simply to painting the play house.

TOOLS AND MATERIALS

Play house

Mineral-fibre roof slates – enough to cover the roof plus half as much again and one extra row of slates

Craft knife

Metal straight edge

2 × 19mm (3/4in) nails per slate

Hammer

2 pairs of louvered shutters to fit the windows (choose a larger size if the exact size is not available)

Hacksaw

8 non-ferrous hinges

4 door magnets

Oil-based paint

5cm (2in) decorating brush

Polyurethane varnish

Baby ridge tiles to cover the length of the ridge

Sand and cement ready mix

Cement board

Trowel

Decorative fascia pre-cut from MDF (medium-density fibre-board) or a strip of MDF and a jigsaw to cut your own fascia (see template at back of book)

Saw

A3 paper for pattern making

Electric drill with screwdriver attachment

FIXING THE ROOF SLATES

Work out how many slates you need for each row. If the slates don't fit the exact width, place as many whole slates in the bottom row as it will take, then cut two equal strips of slate to fill in at each end. Score and snap each slate in half widthways. Fix into position by hammering the nails through the pre-drilled holes and roofing felt. The next row of slates will completely cover the first row of half slates. Arrange them so the side edge of each slate runs down the centre of the slate below it. Fix in position as before. Position the third row so that the slates lie across the width in the same way as the first row. The bottom of the third row should line up with the top of the first row of half slates. Lay the fourth row like the second row, and so on.

FIXING THE SHUTTERS

Remove the window pane divides. If the shutters are larger than the window opening, cut the opening to fit using a hacksaw. Fix the shutters using hinges, re-use the window divides as shutter stops and fix the door magnets.

DECORATING

Paint the play house with oil-based paint and allow to dry for four hours in fine weather. Then finish with a coat of polyurethane varnish.

ADDING THE RIDGE TILES

Mix up the sand and cement according to the manufacturer's instructions. Fill each end of each ridge tile with the mixture and "butter" some along the length. Bed into position.

ADDING THE FASCIA

Cut the fascia to length with the saw. Make a paper pattern of the top point of the roof and use it to cut the fascia ends to this angle. Paint the fascia and fix into position by pre-drilling pilot holes, then nailing it to the front edge of the roof.

ABOVE: *The original play house had a simple wood finish which had been treated for rot.*

ABOVE: *The roof slates and shutters are in position and the play house has been decorated with an oil-based paint.*

ABOVE: *The original window divides have been reused as shutter stops and door magnets fixed in place to hold the shutters closed.*

Water Features

Of all garden fixtures, water features must be the most entrancing. The gentle sound of water trickling, pattering or gurgling has a wonderfully relaxing effect and the glinting, reflective surface brings a new dimension to the garden. It doesn't have to be a grand affair – there is room for a water feature in even the smallest back yard. At its simplest, it could be just a pipe, gently splashing water onto a pile of pebbles below. Water features can range from a miniature fountain bubbling up through pebbles to a nature-inspired pond that would be at home in a cottage-style garden. In between are formal ponds that can be round, rectangular or even T-shaped.

ABOVE: *A formal geometric pond with oriental overtones makes a charming focal point in a terraced town garden.*

Whatever your choice, the water should be kept moving to prevent it from becoming stagnant and that means organizing a small pump to circulate and re-use the water. Submersible pumps can be placed at the bottom of ponds, and some wall masks come ready fitted with a pump. You will also need to have electricity available where you want to site the water feature, so it is best to plan this before the garden is landscaped

LEFT: *This water feature has been planned as part of the garden architecture and is set within a brick-built arch on the wall, which has then been lined with pebbles for a rich texture.*

or paviours laid. Electricity should always be installed by a qualified electrician.

Once the electricity is in position, putting in a pond is not beyond anyone who is handy around the house, especially if you use a ready-made liner. There is a choice of pre-moulded fibreglass linings and the more easily disguised flexible butyl rubber or plastic sheeting. Once the liner is in situ, you can cover the edges with rocks, pebbles and clever planting.

It is best not to site the pond under overhanging branches, as autumn leaves will fall into it, contaminating the pond as they decay.

If you have small children, opt for a water feature that does not form any depth of water (such as one that drains through pebbles) as a toddler can drown in just a few inches of water. Even if you want to plan a larger pool, you could always fill it with pebbles, letting the fountain splash over those until the children are older and the pebbles can be removed.

RIGHT: *An enchanting little pond, complete with fountain and cherub, mimics designs on a much grander scale.*

Mini-pond in a Pot

This delightful miniature pond, complete with water-lily, has been made in a glazed pot that adds a lovely touch when "planted" in the herbaceous border.

TOOLS AND MATERIALS

Large, glazed ceramic pot, at least 40cm (15in) deep
Miniature water-lily

Choose a pot without a drainage hole. Partly fill with water. Put the water-lily still in its pot into the bottom, then fill with water.

Storage

Gardening brings with it an extraordinary amount of practical paraphernalia. Tools, pots and planters, potting compost, raffia, string, seeds and baskets are but a few of the bulky and space-consuming examples. For tools and equipment, garden sheds are the classic solution that most gardens can accommodate, though smaller gardens may be restricted to a mini-shed or tool store, which can be as small as 30cm (12in) deep and so can be tucked into a corner. Sheds can become an attractive part of the garden architecture if painted and decorated.

LEFT: *A pretty little wire shelving unit, intertwined with clematis, makes a delightful garden detail that serves a practical purpose too, providing storage for pots, string, secateurs and wire.*

Another solution is to put your goods on show. Garden pots can be very visual and, displayed on all-weather shelves, can become part of the decorative appeal of the garden. This is an excellent solution for very small gardens and patios, all of which still need space for the practicals. Instead of buying ready-made garden shelving, you could build your own from timber and treat it with exterior-quality paint. Metal shelves old and new can be given a new life using car spray paint or specially manufactured metal paint, which can even be sprayed straight over old rust. All shelves should be fixed firmly to the garden wall – avoid fixing to the house wall as this could lead to damp problems. Once fitted, use the shelves for displays, to store tools, or for bringing on young seedlings, which can look delightful potted up in ranks of terracotta.

LEFT: *There was no room for a greenhouse or even a cold frame in this tiny 6m (20ft) garden, so a "cupboard" was fixed to the outside of the house window, and given a pair of outward-opening windows. This solution provides perfect protection for young seedlings, which can be tended from inside as well as outside. Shelving underneath this outdoor glass cupboard makes a good second home for the plants as they harden off.*

ABOVE: *Old clay pots make a decorative corner display on a blue-painted plant stand.*

ABOVE: *Shelving can be used for purely decorative purposes outside as well as in. Here, simple pebbles, arranged on a blue-painted shelf mounted on corbels, make a charming decorative detail in the garden.*

LEFT: *French baker's shelves make an attractive garden nursery for growing seedlings on.*

Garden Furniture

Furnishing the garden gives you somewhere to sit and relax and, at the same time, adds to the architectural element. Some furniture, like traditional stone furniture, is designed to be an almost permanent part of the garden; certainly it is not meant to be moved with regularity. Architecturally, it provides another step up, its legs almost representing balustrades. And while these wonderful garden fixtures aren't really within most people's price brackets, a similar role is played by old wooden garden benches which, as they weather to a soft green-tinged grey, take on a permanent air as part of the garden architecture.

Single benches exude a peaceful air, probably because they are not conducive to conversation but are more for sitting and contemplating. Love seats, designed in an S-shape, are far more sociable since the occupants sit facing each other. Groups of tables and chairs represent social times in the garden, whether you are simply eating outside with the family, taking tea with a friend or having a party. Permanent outdoor furniture can be made of wood, metal or plastic. Also decorative – and comfortable – outdoors, but not really weatherproof, are wicker and Lloyd loom.

LEFT: *This delightful metal bench was given a new lease of life when it was painted a bright Mediterranean blue. The colour works particularly well here, as it complements the marvellous cascades of purple wisteria.*

ABOVE: *This modern wrought-iron furniture takes reference from French styles of the last century, the elegant, lightweight lines of which are now enjoying another revival.*

LEFT: *Elaborate cast-iron furniture became very popular in Victorian times and its popularity has not really waned . . . though its price means you are more likely to see it in public places than in people's homes.*

RIGHT: *An old Lloyd loom chair was given a fresh look a few years ago with two shades of blue spray-on car paint. Even though the finish is now rather worn, the chair exudes a comfortable, cottagy feel.*

A Lick of Paint

Co-ordinating furniture with its surroundings helps to give the garden a harmonious ambience. By painting old furniture, you can also keep the costs down, as you can pick up bargain pieces from junk shops or simply rejuvenate old kitchen chairs which are due for replacement. And you can be sure of perfect toning as paints come in literally hundreds of shades. These two pairs of chairs were most unprepossessing when they were picked up: the slatted ones were peeling and the Tyrolean style were finished with a tired old varnish.

LEFT: *Clashing Caribbean colours in pink and tangerine make for a lively look in a brightly coloured garden.*

ABOVE: *Taupe and white make an elegant combination for a chair that takes on Italian-style flair. It is an ideal finish for a garden that features a lot of the natural wooden tones.*

ABOVE RIGHT: *The shape of this chair is reminiscent of traditional Tyrolean design, so this has been enhanced by the choice of colours and decoration. These shades also naturally complement the colours of a summer garden.*

RIGHT: *The same chair is given a bright, modern finish to team with the painted shed wall behind. It also co-ordinates well with the silver-grey foliage and lipstick-pink flowers.*

Mosaic Garden Table

This striking mosaic table has been made from bits of broken old china pots and chipped decorative tiles, yet with clever colour co-ordination and a simple, clear design, it makes the most attractive, weatherproof garden furniture around. Although it is resilient to damp, bring it in during very rainy periods and over the winter.

PREPARATION

Mark out the circle using a pair of compasses made from a piece of string tied to a drawing pin at one end and a pencil at the other. Push the drawing pin into the centre of the plywood, ensure that the string is 60cm (2ft) long, then draw the circle. Cut out using a jigsaw.

TOOLS AND MATERIALS

25mm (1in) plywood at least 122 × 122cm (4 × 4ft)
String
Pencil
Drawing pin
Jigsaw
Wood primer
Brush
Plenty of broken china
Tile nippers
Tile adhesive
Tile grout
Grout colour, optional
Plastic gloves
Washing-up brush

1 *Draw the design on the plywood circle, adjusting the string length of the compasses to draw the concentric circles.*

2 *Prime the table with wood primer. Allow to dry according to the manufacturer's instructions.*

3 *Snip pieces of china to fit the design and try it out on the table top.*

4 *Mix up the tile adhesive according to the manufacturer's instructions and "butter" it onto the "inside" of each piece of china before fixing in position.*

5 *Once the design is complete, mix up the grout and colour, if colour is desired. Wearing plastic gloves, use your fingers to work the grout in between all the china pieces. Using a washing-up brush, continue to work the grout in, then clean off any excess.*

Garden Console

This indoor console table has been given an outdoor paint treatment for a witty touch in the garden. It is fun to accessorize it as an indoor side table, as here, or to use it for drinks or serving dishes when entertaining outside.

TOOLS AND MATERIALS

Console table
Medium-grade sandpaper
White acrylic wood primer
5cm (2in) decorating brush
Masonry paint
Artist's acrylic paints in terracotta and pink
Small decorating brush
Fine masonry paint
Acrylic scumble glaze
Water for thinning
Cloth
Sheet of A4 tracing paper
Pencil
Craft knife
Stencil card
Stencil brush
Polyurethane varnish

1 *Thoroughly sand all the surfaces. Prime with white acrylic wood primer. Allow to dry. Tint masonry paint with terracotta paint and use as base coat. Allow to dry for four to six hours.*

2 *Tint fine masonry paint with pink acrylic paint and thin with scumble glaze and water. Paint on and rub off in the direction of the grain. Allow to dry.*

3 *Using the template at the back of the book, trace and cut a leaf stencil from card. Using the terracotta paint, stencil leaves onto the table. Allow to dry, then varnish.*

Getting Comfortable

In high summer, there is nothing more enjoyable than lounging around in the garden, and this is where the softer, more reclining types of furniture come in. The lounger is the lotus-eater's dream – more day bed than chair. Wood-slatted steamer chairs were the original loungers, designed for use on long voyages. Their modern-day equivalent – in wood, metal or plastic – would be given an upholstered cushion. Hammocks are another kind of day bed and, gently swaying between a pair of trees, they would challenge anyone to stay awake. Other, softer "furniture" includes canvas types – deck-chairs and directors' chairs – and even thick tartan picnic rugs and plastic-backed canvas cushions for getting comfortable on picnics.

RIGHT: *A hammock strung between two trees is perfect for whiling away lazy summer days.*

ABOVE: *Given a footrest and, perhaps, a cushion, even wooden outdoor furniture can be truly relaxing. Add a trug of flowers on a side table for the lived-in feel.*

ABOVE: *This witty, plastic-covered, Louis XIV chair offers indoor comfort outside.*

Decorative Deck-chairs

There is little in the way of garden furniture to beat deck-chairs. Their sheer loungeability, foldability and even refurbishability simply can't be bettered! You can buy striped chair canvases ready to nail on, but why not go a step or two further and add some pattern to a plain canvas. It really is not difficult, even if you have never considered yourself to be a dab hand with the paintbrush. One of these designs was made with a ready-cut stencil, the other one was inspired by out-of-copyright bird motif designs, which are reproduced at the back of the book.

TOOLS AND MATERIALS FOR THE "INDIAN BIRDS" DESIGN

Deck-chair
1.5m (5ft) length deck-chair canvas
Decorative outdoor woodstain for chair frame
Small decorating brush
Sheet of A4 tracing paper
Soft and hard pencil
Soft fabric pens in red, green, purple, yellow and blue
Ruler
Masking tape
White cloth
Iron
12 dome-headed upholstery tacks

TOOLS AND MATERIALS FOR THE "STENCILLED RUG" DESIGN

Deck-chair, canvas, and woodstain as for "Indian Birds" design
Small decorating brush
Ready-cut stencil
Masking tape
Stencil brush
Stencil paints in red, ochre, olive and aqua
White cloth
Iron
12 dome-headed upholstery tacks

"INDIAN BIRDS" DESIGN

Wash, rinse, dry and iron the canvas to remove any dressing. Remove the old deck-chair cover and paint the frame with a decorative outdoor stain. Using the tracing paper, trace the bird motifs. Using a soft pencil, scribble densely on the back. Place this side down in the desired position on the canvas and transfer the bird by drawing over the trace lines with a sharp pencil. You will probably then have to go over the lines again on the canvas. Using the soft fabric pens, colour in the birds. For the border, measure 2cm (¾in) from each edge of the canvas and place masking tape the full length of the canvas. Draw a wavy line down the full length, then, using a contrasting pen, fill in the edges so a little canvas shows either side of the wavy line. Repeat for the inside borders, first placing masking tape either side of each border. When dry, set the ink by covering with a white cloth and pressing with the iron at its hottest setting, covering each part for at least two minutes. Use upholstery tacks to fix the canvas securely to the top and bottom of the chair.

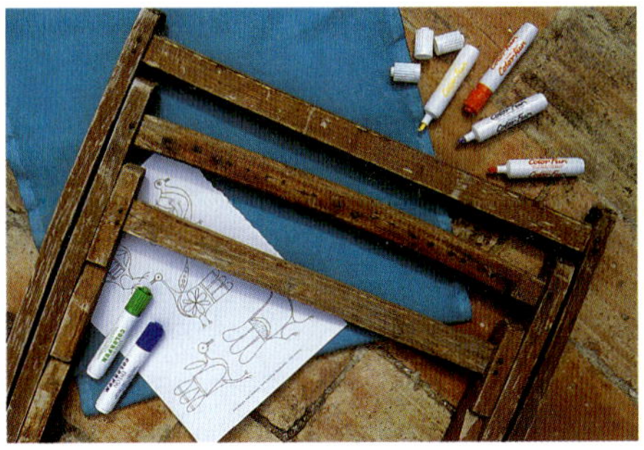

LEFT: *Woodstain, a length of vivid canvas and some soft fabric pens are all you need to revitalize an old deck-chair.*

"STENCILLED RUG" DESIGN

Prepare the canvas and the deck-chair as for the "Indian Birds" design. Plan the design. This one is made up of three motifs: the central motif, a tiny arrowhead, and a cross bordered by lines at the top and bottom. The cross and lines motif make up the border, butting one up to the other. The arrowheads are positioned inside that and the three large motifs placed centrally. Work out the areas of the design before you start. Starting with the borders, fix the stencil in position using masking tape. Load the stencil brush with paint and remove the excess by dabbing up and down on a piece of newspaper until there is hardly any paint left on the brush. Apply this colour to the relevant part of the stencil. Move the stencil and repeat until all areas of that colour have been painted. Using a fresh colour, reposition the stencil over the original colour and apply. Repeat until the design is complete. Set the paint and fix the canvas to the chair as for the "Indian Birds" design.

LEFT: *Stencilling is a very quick way of creating a very individual deck-chair.*

ACCESSORIES AND DECORATIONS

When it comes to style, it is the details that count – the individual choice of decorations that express your personality. Be they large or small, these are the treats that add the finishing touches.

OPPOSITE: *Geraniums in clashing shades of red and pink are set off to perfection in a terracotta pot painted with stripes of vivid colour.*

Outdoor Decorations

Sculpture is the classic outdoor art form. However, if either money to spend on garden decorations or space is limited, then there are other alternatives. Anything that adds structure and form to the garden can be used. Plant pots and containers can be part of the decorations: the traditional example is the classic urn. But you don't even have to go that far. Ordinary pots, painted or carefully arranged in groups, can make a statement, as can unusual containers. Think of some unusual hanging baskets: for example, a colander, basket or bucket, or gather potted plants into a spectacular container, such as an old wheelbarrow, to make a display.

You could choose more purely decorative ideas, such as whirligigs, windchimes, driftwood or pebble collections. Or you can fashion your own decorations – motifs such as hearts or stars made from twigs and branches, wire or raffia.

LEFT: *This inexpensive, painted bamboo birdcage, filled with potted pinks, makes a simple yet charming ornament.*

LEFT: *A merry group of drilled limpets hung on strong thread makes an attractive, joyous windchime.*

ABOVE: *Even simple galvanized shapes take on decorative appeal when given a coat of paint.*

OPPOSITE: *An old wicker mannequin teamed with a miniature wirework version make witty and unexpected garden decorations.*

Hearts in the Garden

Hearts hold universal appeal and there is no reason why they shouldn't find a home in the garden. You will be surprised by what you can make from the most rudimentary weatherproof materials. Garden wire, chicken wire, twigs and raffia are all ideal. The beauty of the heart shape is that it is very easy to achieve. A circle of wire soon becomes a heart when the centre is given a dip and the end a point. Twigs can be coaxed into curves to make two halves, then bound together top and bottom.

RIGHT: *A simple chickenwire heart decorated and suspended with paper string makes a pretty decoration for a sheltered spot.*

ABOVE: *This heart-shaped wreath carries a seasonal message. The twig framework is wound around with variegated ivy and red berries, with a Christmas rose to finish.*

ABOVE: *A heart made from garden wire is given a more decorative texture by knotting natural raffia dyed green and ochre all around the shape.*

Wire Heart

This delightful filigree heart is not difficult to make from ordinary garden wire and it is certainly robust enough to withstand a winter outside. It is composed of several smaller hearts bent into shape with household pliers, then wired together in a beautiful all-over design. Make just one and hang it in a tree, or make several in different sizes or even from different wires. Then group them together on a wall or fence for a delightful display.

TOOLS AND MATERIALS

Wire cutters
Pliers
Medium-gauge garden wire
Florist's wire or fuse wire
Raffia for hanging

1 *Make several small heart shapes in various sizes by cutting short pieces of wire. Using the pliers, bend to a V-shape halfway along each piece and into a curl at either end.*

2 *To make the large heart shape, cut two lengths of garden wire. Using the pliers, bend one piece into a curve for the top of the heart and form a loop at each end. Bend the second piece into a V-shape and form a loop at each end. Link the loops together to join the two pieces. Lay the small hearts inside the large one as you make them, until they fill the shape.*

3 *Using florist's or fuse wire, bind the smaller hearts to the large heart and to each other where they touch, until the whole ensemble is stable. Make a hanger from raffia.*

Garden Sculpture

The classic garden decoration is sculpture: for centuries, stone statues, busts and fountains have graced formal and less formal gardens, providing focal points at the end of vistas or charming finds in secluded spots. The classic Greek and Roman figures are still popular, along with baroque-style cherubs and putti (little boys). Originals in stone, aged by lichens, natural salts and the passage of time, highlighting detail and combining to create a patina, are exquisite but usually prohibitively expensive. However, the ageing process can be accelerated on modern stone versions by coating them with natural yoghurt and keeping them in damp, shady places.

Beautiful as the traditional forms of sculpture are, there are alternatives that may be far more relevant to

LEFT: *A rusty wheel and mannequin's hand create a faintly sinister sculpture that is reflected in a mirror set against the garden wall. A tiny, diamond-shaped mirror hangs between, twisting, turning and glinting in the sun to give the whole ensemble a dynamic quality.*

LEFT: *Metal and water provide a fascinating, dynamic sculpture that is a cross between a birdbath and a water feature.*

OPPOSITE: *An exquisite male torso, turned modestly towards the wall, provides art and structure to the side of a garden.*

your garden and far more personal to you. Metal and wire sculpture is fashionable nowadays and works very well outside, as does willow, woven into dynamic figures. Mosaic, too, can be a lovely medium for sculpture as it quickly transforms all sorts of unpromising bits of paraphernalia.

Plants themselves can become sculpture, such as in topiary, where generally small-leaved evergreens are clipped into spirals, cones, orbs and animals. It is a long process as the shrubs take time to grow, but some garden centres sell them already started and all you have to do is keep them trimmed to shape.

OPPOSITE: *Even a rusty old chair frame can become sculpture. This one, flanked on all sides by neatly trimmed trees, is given throne-like importance.*

LEFT: *Classical-style statues make elegant focal points, set at the end of vistas.*

ABOVE: *Old galvanized baths and bowls have been wittily decorated with ceramic chips cut from broken china, a couple of old teacups and ginger-jar tops.*

ABOVE: *Evergreens clipped into simple topiary shapes make classic living sculptures that need not be over-grand. Kept to a smaller scale in pots, they become enchanting details in any garden.*

Decorating Pots

Transforming an ordinary terracotta pot or simple galvanized bucket into something special really doesn't have to be difficult. There are so many media to choose from that it is an easy matter to find one that suits you. You may be happy with paint applied in bold geometric patterns or simple motifs. If you are skilled with the brush, you might like to try something a little more figurative. Another easy option is to stick small objects onto your pots – ceramic chips, perhaps, to make a mosaic or shells arranged in a simple, textural pattern.

OPPOSITE: *Simple patterns in co-ordinated ceramic chips make for striking mosaic garden pots.*

LEFT: *Plain terracotta pots painted in clear Mediterranean greens and blues and planted with scarlet geraniums and sweet-smelling thyme will enliven even the dullest corner of the garden or patio.*

ABOVE: *Terracotta pots colour-washed in springtime shades of yellow and green are ideal for a display of daffodils and crocuses.*

LEFT: *This pot has been given a necklace of weathered glass "beads" dangling on wires from a main wire fixed under the rim of the pot.*

Mexican Painted Pots

A series of basic motifs painted over stripes of vibrant colours gives simple pots a rich Mexican look. It is lovely to let some of the untreated terracotta colour show through, especially if you use pots with a fluted top like this one. Planted up with geraniums in hot summer colours and stacked together they make a lively garden feature.

TOOLS AND MATERIALS

Fluted-top garden pot
Masking tape
White undercoat
Small decorating brush
Gouache poster colours
2 artist's brushes, one very fine
Polyurethane varnish

1 *Mark the stripes on the pot using masking tape. Cut some lengths into narrower widths to get variation in the finished design. Bear in mind that the areas covered by masking tape will remain natural terracotta.*

2 *Completely paint the main body of the pot with undercoat. Allow to dry according to the manufacturer's instructions.*

3 *Paint the coloured stripes, changing colour after each band of masking tape. Allow to dry completely.*

4 *Peel off the masking tape to reveal coloured stripes alternating with terracotta stripes.*

5 *Using the fine artist's brush and the undercoat, paint simple motifs over the stripes. When completely dry, coat with varnish.*

Verdigris Bucket

There is something irresistible about the luminous, blue-green tones of verdigris. It is a colour that always complements plants and is not difficult to reproduce on a cheap, galvanized bucket. To make the rust bucket shown behind the verdigris one, follow the steps below, but substitute rust-coloured acrylic paint for the aqua.

TOOLS AND MATERIALS

Galvanized bucket
Medium-grade sandpaper
Metal primer
Small decorating brush
Gold paint
Large artist's brush
Amber shellac
Artist's acrylic paint in white and aqua
Water for mixing
Natural sponge
Polyurethane varnish

1 *Sand the bucket, then prime with metal primer. Allow to dry for two to three hours. Paint with gold paint and allow to dry for two to three hours.*

2 *Paint with amber shellac and allow to dry for 30 minutes. Mix white acrylic paint with aqua-green and enough water to make a watery consistency.*

3 *Sponge the verdigris paint on and allow to dry for one to two hours. Apply a coat of varnish.*

Lead Chimney

The wonderful chalky tones of lead have made it a popular material for garden containers down the centuries. But lead is incredibly heavy and very expensive, so here is a way of faking it, using a plastic, terracotta-coloured chimney and some simple paint effects.

TOOLS AND MATERIALS

Plastic, terracotta-coloured chimney
Sandpaper
Acrylic primer
Large artist's brush
Charcoal-grey emulsion
Acrylic scumble glaze
White emulsion
Water
Decorating brush
Polyurethane varnish

1 *Sand the chimney to give it a key. Paint with one coat of acrylic primer and allow to dry for one to two hours.*

2 *Apply one coat of charcoal-grey emulsion and allow to dry for two to three hours.*

3 *Tint the scumble glaze with white emulsion and thin with water. Paint over the chimney randomly. Wash over with water and allow to dry.*

4 *Add more of the white scumble mixture to parts of the chimney for extra colour and "age". Varnish with polyurethane varnish.*

Functional Decorations

The very paraphernalia of gardens can be decorative. An old garden fork, its handle polished with use, a galvanized watering can, turned soft grey with time, or a wheelbarrow, pitted with wear, all have attractive forms that give structure to the garden. Somehow, the balance and symmetry necessary for tools to be efficient at their job usually also result in shapes that are easy on the eye. They have reassuring associations, too: they remind us that people are nearby. So let them loiter around the garden; leave them where they were last used and they will reward you with their ever-changing decorative appeal.

ABOVE: *Sundials may not be moveable decorations, but their original* raison d'être *reminds us that these are not fripperies. They were clearly more necessary in centuries gone by than they are today, but they still exude a functional quality that is honest and pleasing.*

LEFT: *Even old garden tools make decorative garden ornaments, left just where they were last used.*

LEFT: *An old watering can, its curves reminiscent of a vintage car, provides a simple structure left by the garden bed.*

Twigwam

Plant supports are functional – but that doesn't mean they can't be decorative, too. This one, made from branches pruned from garden trees interwoven with willow, makes a charming structural detail in the flower beds. Alternatively, it can be used to support clematis or any other climber for a wonderful, free-standing, outdoor floral display.

TOOLS AND MATERIALS

3 unbranched poles, about 91cm (3ft) long
String or willow for tying
3 unbranched poles, about 30cm (12in) long
Plenty of fine, freshly cut willow branches

1 *Stand up the three taller poles to form a "wigwam" and tie them together at the top with string or willow.*

2 *Stand the three shorter poles between the longer ones and tie them in the same way. Start to weave the willow branches in and out of all the poles, working upwards from the bottom.*

3 *Once enough of the wigwam has been woven to keep the shorter poles securely in position, untie the top fastening. Continue weaving until the shorter poles are almost covered.*

Chickenwire Cloche

This quirky chickenwire cloche can be used to protect plants from slugs and birds or simply "planted" into the flowerbed as a charming and original miniature obelisk.

TOOLS AND MATERIALS

Wire cutters
Fine-mesh chickenwire
Pliers
Medium-gauge garden wire

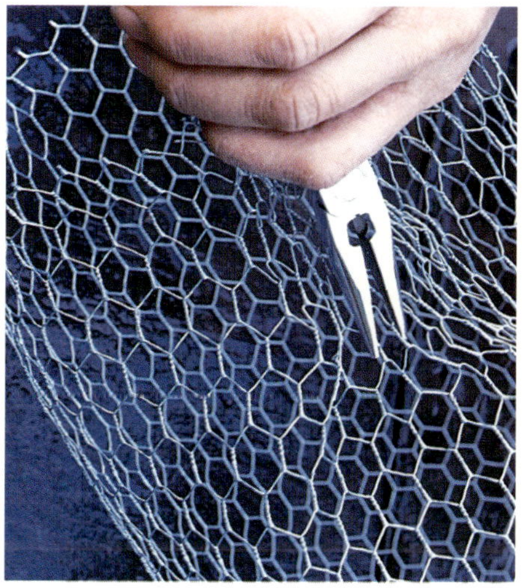

1 *Using the wire cutters, cut a piece of chickenwire about 50 × 50cm (20 × 20in). Roll it to form a tube, making sure the twisted sides of each lozenge shape run vertically. Join the tube by twisting the cut ends of the wire around each other, using either your fingers – with due care – or the pliers, whichever you find easier.*

2 *Use the pliers to squeeze together each lozenge shape. At the top, to about 7.5cm (3in) from the top, squeeze each lozenge as tightly as it will go. Then continue to pinch the holes down the tube, allowing the holes to become larger and larger until the fullest part has been reached. At the bottom end, make a "skirt" by squeezing the lozenges.*

3 *Wind garden wire tightly around the top of the cloche to finish.*

Pretty Effects in Practical Areas

Vegetable patches needn't be the Cinderellas of the garden. There is something voluptuous about burgeoning fruits and first-class vegetables and there is something appealing about the structures they need to climb up. So make a virtue of your vegetable gardens, whether you plan to give them their own special space or let them fraternize with the flowers.

LEFT: *There is something appealing about pea sticks, in that the twiggy branches give the appearance of a wild hedgerow up which the peas are scrambling. There is a practical element, too: the twigs offer plenty of climbing support.*

LEFT: *Soldier-like bamboo canes take on an even more regimental appearance with their labels tied uniformly along the line.*

ABOVE: *Keeping track of plant labels can be well-nigh impossible once the plants are growing and overflowing their original sites, so turn them into a decoration in themselves. Cut out a board from plywood, giving it a decorative motif at the top, such as these tulips. Paint it in bright colours, screw in some hooks and you have an attractive garden record of what you have planted.*

OPPOSITE: *Whether it is fruit, vegetables or seedlings you want to protect, make a witty scarecrow to double as an amusing garden sculpture. This dapper chap with handtool hands and a colander face, wears a sporty panama hat.*

Chicken Box Plant Stand

It is fun, especially in spring when the plants are low, to hoist a few flowers on high. And here is a witty way to achieve that: make a decorative chicken nesting on a box, raise it on a stake and fill the box with pots of seasonal flowers. Use it to bring colour to any patchy part of the garden, wherever that may be as the year progresses.

TOOLS AND MATERIALS

Sheet of A3 tracing paper
Soft pencil
Sheet of A3 paper
Scissors
MDF (medium-density fibreboard), measuring about 60 × 60cm (2 × 2ft)
Jigsaw
25mm (1in) plywood, measuring at least 76 × 45cm (30 × 18in)
6 screws
Screwdriver
Undercoat
Small decorating brush
Model-painting enamel in red, orange, white, blue, black and green
Artist's brush
5 × 7.5cm (2 × 3in) post, about 122cm (4ft) long

1 *Using the template at the back of the book, make a paper pattern for the chicken. Draw around the chicken shape on the MDF. Cut out using a jigsaw. Cut three pieces of plywood measuring 17 × 9cm ($6\frac{3}{4} \times 3\frac{1}{2}$in) and one measuring 17 × 5cm ($6\frac{3}{4} \times 2$in).*

2 *Screw the larger panels onto the chicken, one on either side. Screw the narrower, bottom panel between them. Screw the final plywood panel onto the front.*

3 *Paint both sides of the chicken and the box with undercoat. Allow to dry according to the manufacturer's instructions.*

4 *Sketch the chicken details onto both sides of the chicken shape and, using model-painting enamel, add the colours. Allow to dry overnight.*

5 *Paint the box green. Allow to dry for three hours. Screw the post to the back of the box.*

Living in the Garden

The real joy of a garden is to be able to relax outside with friends and family in your own private outdoor room. With space to relax, entertain and play, the garden will be ready for you whenever you feel like a breath of fresh air.

Opposite: *A miniature garden room in itself, an awning is invaluable when the sun is hot, the weather is gusty or if your garden lacks privacy.*

Comfortable Living Areas

If you set up a comfortable living area in the garden, you are much more likely to use it. With table and chairs standing ready, it is so much easier to bring the coffee and rolls out for breakfast al fresco. With an area set aside for the children, they will much more readily run outside to play. The priority is to earmark a sheltered living area with a cosy, room-like feel. If it is not next to the house, it will need to be screened by hedges or trellis to lend a sense of privacy. You don't need a large space – just think how cramped restaurants are, yet once seated, you feel comfortable.

Once the living area is established, try to incorporate something that stimulates each of the senses. Place a handsome specimen plant within view of the seating area or position the chairs to look onto a pleasant vista. Nature will offer plenty to please your ear: summer birdsong, the hum of bees and the whisper of trees and shrubs gently stirred by a breeze can be enhanced by the music of windchimes, and a water feature can offer the relaxing sound of trickling water.

For fragrance, site plants with richly perfumed blooms near the seating area. Old-fashioned roses and honeysuckle are hard to beat or try aromatic lavender and rosemary. Many flowers exude their scent at night. Summer jasmine and tobacco plants (nicotiana) are two favourites. For touch, you can plant a contrast of textures from feathery love-in-a-mist and shapely ferns to rich succulents. Finally, taste can be stimulated by nearby aromatic herbs or fragrant fruits such as strawberries and blackberries.

Above: *Lunch taken outside in the summer can be a memorable occasion. Attractive garden furniture and a pretty wild flower arrangement create a restful ambience, while fresh fruits and salads look wonderful set out on colourful china.*

Above: *Throw a blue-checked cloth over the garden table, add some seasonal potted arrangements and you have the perfect setting for drinks outside, even on a fresh but sunny early spring day.*

ABOVE: *Swathes of roses on a trellis at the back and over archways to each side provide a fragrant and intimate screen for a picturesque seating area.*

LEFT: *Part of the enjoyment of being outside is having a view to admire. This seating area on the patio next to the house overlooks an almost classical vista in an urban garden.*

Awnings and Umbrellas

Living outside sometimes requires shelter and shade, be it from the wind or a blistering sun. On a windy day a windbreak of some kind will enable you to sit outside even in early spring or early autumn, when it would otherwise be impossible. A capacious sun umbrella, on the other hand, will allow you to dine outside or simply relax under its shelter even in the middle of the day in high summer.

RIGHT: *A dead tree provided the inspiration for a sheltered seating area in this garden. The natural awning was constructed from the pruned branches, while a dovecote on the top introduces the gentle cooing of doves.*

ABOVE: *Take two chairs and one umbrella and you immediately have a pleasantly informal seating arrangement and a moveable sheltered spot from which to enjoy the garden.*

ABOVE: *Late summer jobs, such as topping and tailing fruit, become pleasurable pastimes under an awning. Original Edwardian awnings like this one come with a lightweight metal frame that is easily erected and the awning is simply slipped over.*

Windchime

The charm of this shell windchime lies in its simplicity. Garden ornaments need to be visually striking as they will be viewed from some distance. In this case, the sand-dollars give the windchime its striking form while the cockle-shells strung on raffia provide the music.

TOOLS AND MATERIALS

Raffia
Scissors
10 pre-drilled cockle-shells
Electric drill with fine drill bit (if you cannot get pre-drilled shells)
3 sand-dollars

1 *Cut three lengths of raffia about 60cm (2ft) long and two 45cm (18in) long. If you can get pre-drilled cockle-shells, so much the better; if not, carefully drill each shell using an electric drill with a fine drill bit. Tie one shell to each end of each length of raffia. Fold all the lengths of raffia in half and gather them together at the halfway point. Thread this loop through the hole in one sand-dollar.*

2 *Feed the ends of the raffia, including the shells, through the loop to tie them to the sand-dollar.*

3 *Feed two further lengths of raffia through the hole in the sand-dollar and tie them together at the top. In the same way, link and tie the other two sand-dollars to the top of the chime.*

Children's Areas

In family homes, gardens are very much for the children. They need their own outdoor space to play in and, where there isn't enough room to run or kick a ball, the best solution is to set aside one area of the garden and build some sort of structure specially for them. They may like a play house, which provides all-weather outdoor play, or they may prefer a climbing frame or a swing and slide. If any of these are well planned, they need not take up too much space. If you are lucky enough to have a suitable tree, you may even be inspired to build a tree house, which wouldn't take up any space at all!

ABOVE: *Play houses can be decorated to enhance the whole garden. They not only offer a private place for imaginative play in the early years and a den as the children get older, but they also provide storage space for bulkier toys such as free-standing kitchens and dolls' houses.*

RIGHT: *These steps up to a platform take children to an exciting assault course slide. The same idea could be adapted for a tree house.*

RIGHT: *A delightful, little crooked house, complete with veranda and chimney, is built on stilts with a short stairway leading up to it. The very stuff of nursery stories, many an hour can be whiled away here in imaginative play.*

BELOW: *Climbing frames made from rustic poles blend happily into the garden. Carefully designed, they can be added to over the years should space allow, or simply adapted to keep the challenge fresh.*

Animal Friends

Even in the densest urban areas, the outdoors is not devoid of wildlife. Countless creatures consider our gardens to be their home, as much as we consider them a part of ours. Many creatures we very much welcome, delighting in watching their activities. And, of course, wild creatures often help to maintain the ecological balance, eating unwanted guests such as greenfly and other pests.

Most wild creatures like to be self-catering and are very happy to organize their own homes, though with a little encouragement, such as the simple provision of a shallow dish of fresh water, they will appreciatively settle on your plot. Some plants attract beneficial insects such as butterflies and bees. The most obvious ones are the more highly scented species such as buddleia (butterfly bush), lavender and honeysuckle. Birds can be encouraged by birdtables in the winter and birdbaths in the summer. Toads, which are consummate devourers of flies, like to set up house in cool, damp places – in flower pots laid on their sides in a leafy, private place, perhaps, or under a pile of stones. Once in residence, they usually stay, gradually working their way through the insect population.

BELOW: *Butterflies can be attracted into the garden by planting their favourite nectar-rich shrubs, such as buddleia and this exquisite pink autumn-flowering sedum.*

ABOVE: *Carefully positioned to catch the mellow afternoon sun, a leafy arbour can become a favourite spot for the resident cat.*

ABOVE: *A dovecote is not only architecturally pleasing, it provides a home for one of the most beautiful species of birds. And they don't even demand to live in the country. These doves moved into a dovecote in a tiny town terrace.*

LEFT: *Birdbaths can take the form of a piece of sculpture. This mosaic structure "nests" in a bed of marigolds and wallflowers.*

Lighting Effects

Enjoying the garden after nightfall is dependent on garden lighting and, in most domestic gardens, that is sadly lacking. If you are having your garden landscaped, you may consider having electricity cables laid and bringing in an expert to work out a proper plan. This would usually include general lighting, plus perhaps some spotlighting for focal points such as a favourite piece of statuary. But even if you don't want to go to that expense, there is a lot you can do.

Before you start, it is worth bearing in mind that, unless you are planning powerful floodlighting, you are unlikely to achieve the light levels you would normally expect inside. And would you want to? Part of the appeal of being outside at night is the moody lighting and the appreciation of the moon and stars.

The easiest solution for general outdoor lighting is to fix a powerful halogen light to the outside of the house. Since the living areas of the garden are usually near the house, this should be ample. Another easy idea is to have an electrician fit an all-weather socket to the outside of the house, taking a spur off the ring main. This can then be used for plugging in both light and sound for fabulous evening entertainment. For special occasions, you may like to hire all-weather strings of lights to hang in the trees. Plain white bulbs are always particularly effective.

ABOVE: *Place outdoor lights under plants with strong architectural shapes to create drama for the garden at night.*

RIGHT: *Outdoor fairy lights woven into the trellis and climber makes a charming decorative effect for summer evenings.*

OPPOSITE: *Spotlights highlighting the statuary and pond provide excellent outdoor lighting for this formal Italianate garden.*

Candle Power

Candles must surely offer the most romantic outdoor lighting. The light they cast is natural, flattering and evocative of campfires. They are also very practical for outside as they don't rely on electricity. There are many forms of candle-light. Ordinary indoor candles can simply be taken outside, candelabra and all, for a candle-lit dinner. If the weather is a touch breezy, use a lantern or some other holder which protects the flame from the elements. Choose lanterns that can take a substantial-sized candle, otherwise you will be forever jumping up and down to light yet another. Also, check that the metalwork is robust, as some imported aluminium lanterns collapse once the lit candle melts the solder holding it together.

As well as lanterns, you could try Victorian night-lights, tumbler-like glass containers that hang on wires, huge glass hanging lanterns, candles in garden pots or galvanized buckets which – once they burn down below the rim – are protected from the wind. Candles that are specially designed to cope with the outside elements are garden flares, which produce a huge flame and can burn for up to three hours. The light they give off is also surprisingly bright, which makes them ideal for general lighting around the entertainment area or for pathway lighting.

The main danger of outdoor candles and garden flares is that the wind does blow the flame, so it is important always to position them well away from any foliage or furniture.

BELOW: *Lanterns provide perfect garden candle-light, as they protect the flame from the wind.*

ABOVE: *Garden flares, "planted" around the garden, provide a surprising amount of light. Many are also scented to discourage insects.*

ABOVE: *Victorian night-lights hung on wires create a romantic glow in the trees.*

RIGHT: *A large, glass, hanging lantern makes enchanting lighting for dinner al fresco. Lotus-like flower candles float above a bed of shells, looking like an exotic lily pond.*

Gilded Pots

Ordinary terracotta pots, gilded and filled with candle wax, offer the most enchanting outdoor lighting. Make several pots in assorted sizes to group on tables, patios, walls and outdoor shelves.

TOOLS AND MATERIALS

Assorted terracotta pots
Red oxide primer
Small decorating brush
Water-based gold size
Gold Dutch metal leaf
Soft cloth
Amber shellac
Artist's acrylic paint in white and aqua
Water for mixing
Artist's brush
Wick
Candle wax
Double boiler

1 Prime each pot with red oxide primer. Allow to dry for three to four hours.

2 Apply a coat of water-based gold size and allow to dry for about 30 minutes or until the size becomes transparent.

3 To apply the gold Dutch metal leaf, lift the sheets carefully and lay them onto the size, gently smoothing each one with a cloth or soft-bristled brush. Brush off any excess leaf and polish with a soft cloth.

4 Apply a coat of amber shellac to seal the metal leaf and allow to dry for 30 minutes.

5 To age the pots, tint a little white acrylic with aqua and thin with water, brush on and rub off with a cloth. Allow to dry for two to three hours. For the candle, suspend the wick in the pot by tying it to a pole laid across the pot. Ensure the wick reaches the bottom of the pot. Slowly melt the wax in a double boiler and pour into the pot. Allow to set overnight.

Entertaining Outside

What a joy it is, when all is said and done, to invite friends over and relax together in the garden. It is the wonderful casualness of al fresco eating that is so appealing. The food can be simple: fresh salads, fruits and vegetables, served with just a little dressing or cream, whichever is appropriate. Meat or fish can simply be grilled or barbecued with fresh herbs, the aroma complementing the scent of the herbs growing in the beds. Some bread, a bottle of wine and you have all the ingredients for a memorable day or evening.

Decorating the table can be effortless – all you need is a table centre of flowers and plants from the garden and candles for an evening party.

BELOW: *With all the gentle outdoor sounds plus the perfume of evening-scented flowers, even the simplest of informal gatherings becomes a special occasion.*

ABOVE: *Teatime, when the heat of the day is over, is a wonderful time to get together in the garden, whether for pure entertainment or to celebrate bringing in the fruit harvest.*

Iron Lantern

Give new aluminium lanterns the more appealing appearance of aged iron. Even the simplest shapes and brashest finishes become infinitely more pleasing when given the well-worn look of a lantern of yore.

TOOLS AND MATERIALS

Masking tape
Metal lantern
Medium-grade sandpaper
White metal primer
Large artist's brush
Silver paint
Small natural sponge
Black emulsion paint
Red oxide artist's acrylic paint
Water for mixing
Flower mister
Satin polyurethane varnish

1 Stick masking tape onto all the glass areas of the lantern. Sand the metal to provide a key. Paint one coat of metal primer onto all the metal parts of the lantern. Allow to dry for two to three hours. Paint on a silver base coat.

2 Dip the natural sponge into black emulsion and dab onto the lantern. Allow to dry for one to two hours.

3 Mix red oxide acrylic paint with a little water and, using the artist's brush, drip this down the lantern at intervals, to resemble rust. Spray with a flower mister. Allow to dry for one to two hours. Varnish, allow to dry and remove the masking tape.

Tablecentres

Outdoor table decorations are the very easiest to put together because they are at their most successful when they complement their surroundings. So plunder the garden and then combine the ingredients with flair. You may cut a few flowers, add foliage or even fruit and vegetables; or you may simply gather together some of the smaller pots from around the garden. The concentration on a table of what grows in naturally looser arrangements throughout the garden serves to focus the overall look.

ABOVE: *Ivy planted in glass-shaped galvanized containers and accessorized with a couple of pastel-painted canes to resemble straws makes a witty cocktail tablecentre.*

LEFT: *In summer, a couple of potted strawberry plants are transformed into a tablecentre when they are contained in a wire jug and accessorized with a few ripe fruits.*

RIGHT: A wire basket interwoven with raffia on its base gathers together pots of verbena surrounded by tiny pots of variegated ivy. The end result is an outdoor casualness perfectly in accord with its surroundings.

BELOW: Ornamental cabbages, complemented by individual cabbage leaves used decoratively on the napkins and a miniature arrangement in a baby jar, make an unusually attractive tablecentre.

Practicalities

Bringing colour into the garden with paints and stains lends impact both to the planting and to the whole garden. You can do this by painting or staining fences, trelliswork, garden buildings, furniture and containers. However, any paint job outdoors has to be able to withstand a lot of beating from the weather – frosts, strong winds, torrential rain and the blistering sun of high summer. For this reason, it is best to use exterior-quality products: they are less likely to peel and flake, their colours are less likely to fade and they are specifically designed to protect the surface they are covering. Having said that, you can achieve a reasonably hard-wearing finish using a wider variety of paints over a primer, then finishing with a polyurethane varnish when decorating items such as pots and containers, which are not crucial to the garden structure.

Whatever you plan to paint or stain, it is important to use compatible primers, undercoats and varnishes, otherwise they may react against each other. So if you plan to use a water-based product, make sure you also prime and finish using water-based products; similarly, acrylics should be kept together and oil-based products should be kept together. Also, ideally, you should stick to one manufacturer's products for each job as that will ensure compatibility. When you are not able to do this, it would be wise to test a small, hidden area first.

ABOVE: *Gilded miniature clay pots, filled with candle wax, will add colour and atmosphere to the garden room.*

Always do any kind of exterior painting on a dry, warm day – and preferably after several similar days, with the prospect of more to come. The reasons for this are clear: if the surface is damp, the paint will not adhere properly. If the surface is hot, from baking sun, it will blister. If frost is about, it will "lift" the paint.

Remember, too, that several thin layers of paint always produce a more enduring and better-looking finish than one thick one.

LEFT: *Wonderful decorative effects can be created using just a few specialist materials, such as emulsion and acrylic paints, water-based gold size and Dutch metal leaf, gilt cream and felt-tipped pens in gold and silver.*

Tools for Painting

You will achieve a more controlled and permanent paint finish if you use the right tools for the job. And, if you are investing in new brushes, it makes sense to care for them by cleaning them correctly.

DECORATING BRUSHES

These are the best brushes to use for applying base coats. For very large, flat surfaces you may need an emulsion brush, but for most tasks a flat brush of around 7–10cm (3–4in) would be adequate. Sash brushes, so called because they are used to paint window frames, are around 3–5cm (1–2in) wide and are indispensable for many of the more fiddly jobs.

TOOLS FOR PAINT EFFECTS

Artist's brushes are useful for creating the more decorative finishes, such as stone, lead and verdigris paint effects. The finer the job, the finer the brush needs to be. Where the lines between one colour and the next need to be merged, the paint should be applied with a natural sponge. To stipple paint, use a special stippling brush or a fine decorating sash brush. For stencilling, you will need a stencil brush which has short stiff bristles. The brush should be used with a dabbing rather than a brushing action to prevent paint seeping under the stencil and spoiling the shape.

CLEANING UP

Brushes used for water-based products can be cleaned using soap and water. Work up a lather right up into the ferrule. Rinse thoroughly until the water runs clear. Squeeze and shake out any excess water, straighten the bristles, then lay on a piece of newspaper. Fold the paper to make a parcel around the bristles, which will restore them to shape and absorb excess moisture. Brushes used for oil-based products should be cleaned using white spirit. Wash out the white spirit using soap and water and dry as above.

LEFT: *(From left to right) stencilling brush, dusting brush (sometimes used for stippling paint surfaces), sash brush, softening brush (used to soften brush strokes before the paint dries), stippling brush, large decorating brush, rubber rocker (used to create wood-grain effects), artist's brushes, flat-bristle varnishing brush, natural sponge, soft cloth.*

Preparation Pays

Whatever job you are doing, make sure the surface is properly prepared first, following the manufacturer's instructions. There are various surface materials in the garden, all of which need different treatments. If you are re-treating any surface, you should use the same type of product; for example, you won't be able to paint over oiled furniture or creosoted wood.

LEFT: *Garden sheds or play houses made of smooth-planed wood can be painted with exterior-quality paints for a fresh, new finish.*

MASONRY

Prepare walls by removing dirt and loose paint with a stiff brush. If the wall is still powdery, seal the surface with a stabilizing solution.

Paint with smooth or textured masonry paint. This is available in hundreds of colours, most of which have to be mixed up specially by the supplier. If you want to use only a small amount, for decorative detailing or, perhaps, a shed wall, you can tint the paint with artist's colour (check a small amount first).

LEFT: *Old wooden furniture, such as deck-chairs, can be given a new lease of life with a coat of coloured wood stain.*

LEFT: *Using masonry paint tinted with artist's colours, exterior house walls can be as vibrant as you wish.*

SMOOTH-PLANED WOOD

Garden doors, garden furniture and some garden buildings such as play houses and sheds are made from smooth-planed wood. There are three types of products you can use to paint these: exterior gloss, exterior woodstain and exterior varnish, which comes in a clear, matt or gloss finish and in a choice of colours. Most woodstains come in wood colours, though some specialist manufacturers produce coloured stains too. Outdoor buildings and furniture are usually bought ready-treated with a preservative which you can paint over. Check this before you buy. Wash the surface with a sugar soap solution, then rinse thoroughly. Rub down with wet and dry paper. Allow to dry out thoroughly, then paint on a coat of exterior primer. Allow to dry, then rub down and apply an undercoat. Allow to dry, then rub down and apply exerior gloss paint. Always allow adequate drying time between each stage, taking the manufacturer's specified time as the absolute minimum.

If you would prefer a finish which allows the grain of the wood to show through, you can choose either a woodstain or a varnish. The colour in woodstains penetrates the wood; varnish, even if it is a stained varnish, sits on top. These products are usually applied directly to the clean, dry wood.

ROUGH-SAWN WOOD

Most garden fencing, trellis, and some garden buildings are made of rough-sawn wood. These need to be treated with a staining product that soaks into the wood, rather than sits on top of it, as a paint or varnish does. Always check the product is suitable for exterior, rough-sawn wood. Most of them come in a wood colour or green, though some specialist manufacturers produce coloured stains. Rough-sawn products are often ready-treated with a preservative when you buy them. Check that the preservative can be overpainted. If the product has not been preserved, use a compatible preservative before coating with stain.

METAL

Metal gates and railings can be painted with exterior-quality gloss paint. Brush previously painted metal with a wire brush to clean it and remove any loose paint and metal badly eroded by rust. Then dust off. Treat rust with a rust cure and prime any new or bare metal with the appropriate metal primer, then allow to dry before applying the top coat. There are also special metal paints available in aerosol and brush-on versions that can be applied straight over the metal without priming, even if rusty. However, remove any loose rust first with a wire brush.

LEFT: *Garden trelliswork doesn't have to be a uniform brown. Here, a soft-blue woodstain offers the perfect backdrop for a pink planting scheme.*

RIGHT: *Treat metal gates and railings to a new coat of exterior gloss or metal paint.*

Templates

Unless indicated otherwise, all the templates and plans are drawn to actual size. To enlarge a template to the correct size, either use a grid system or a photocopier. For the grid system, trace the template and draw a grid of evenly spaced squares over your tracing. To scale up, draw a larger grid onto another piece of paper. Copy the outline onto the second grid by taking each square individually and drawing the relevant part of the outline in the equivalent larger square. To make templates you will need tracing paper, hard and soft pencils, paper or card and scissors.

Pretty Pebble Rug page 30

Design plan

Ideas with Paint, pages 48/9

Leaf motif

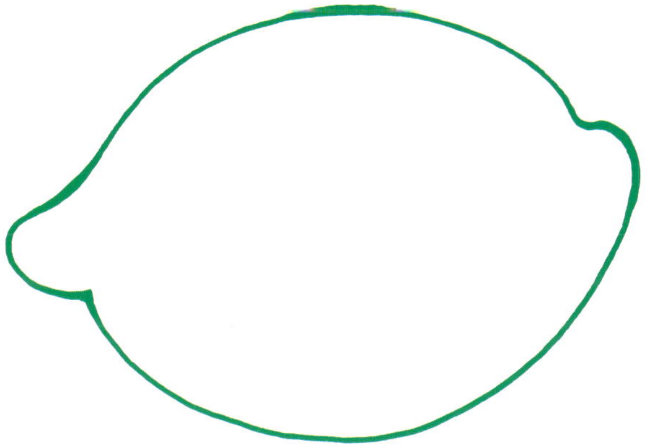

Lemon and lime motif

Lizard motif

Enlarge by 200% for actual size

Customized Play House, pages 88/89

Fascia template

Garden Console, page 100

Leaf motif

Chicken Box Plant Stand, pages 126/127

Enlarge by 200% for actual size

Decorative Deck-chairs, pages 102/103

"Indian Birds" motifs

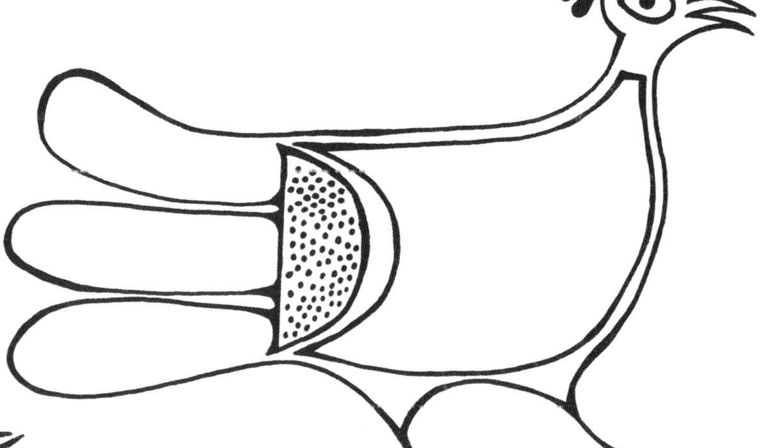

Stockists and Suppliers

PAINTS

Finnigans Hammerite
Hunting Specialised Products Ltd
Prudhoe
Northumberland NE42 6LP
Tel: 01661 830000
Specialized single-coat metal paint, both spray-on and brush-on

Keim Mineral Paints Ltd
Muckley Cross
Morville
Nr Bridgnorth
Shropshire WV16 4RR
Tel: 01746 714543
Specialized exterior paints

Paint Magic Jocasta Innes
79 Shepperton Road
London N1 3DF
Tel: 0171 354 9696
Decorative paint finishes that can be teamed with varnish for light outdoor use

Sadolin Nobel UK Ltd
Sadolin House
Medow Lane
St Ives
Cambridgeshire PE17 4UY
Tel: 01480 496868
Specialized exterior stains in a wide range of colours

PAVINGS

Brett Specialised Aggregates
Sturry Quarry
Fordwich Road
Sturry
Kent CT2 0BW
Tel: 01227 712876

Marshalls Mono
Southowram
Halifax HX3 9SY
Tel: 01422 366666
Natural clay pavings and concrete block paving

Pioneer Supamix
Griff Lane
Griff Clara
Nuneaton
Warwickshire CV10 7PP
Tel 01203 351251
Pebbles and aggregates

Town & Country Pavings
Unit 10 Shrubland Nurseries
Round Stone Lane
Angmering
West Sussex BN16 4AT
Tel: 01903 776297

GARDEN STATUARY

Drummonds of Bramley
Birtley Farm
Horsham Road
Bramley
Guildford
Surrey GU5 0LA
Tel: 01483 898766
Architectural salvage

Wallace Antiques
High Street
Cuckfield
West Sussex RH17 5JX
Tel: 01444 415006
Antique garden statuary and furniture

GARDEN ARCHITECTURE

Agriframes
Charlwoods Road
East Grinstead
West Sussex RH19 2HG
Tel: 01342 328644
Metal arches, bowers, obelisks, pergolas, flower screens, gazebos, walkways, garden ornaments, greenhouses and watering accessories

Anthony de Grey Trellises
Broadhinton Yard
77a North Street
London SW4 0HQ
Tel 0171 738 8866
Five different kinds of trellis available in panels and as rose arches, archways, arbours, planters, pavilions, gazebos – all in a range of colours

Matthew Eden Garden Furniture
Pickwick End
Corsham
Wiltshire SN13 0JB
Tel: 01249 713335
Wirework arches, domes, walkways and furniture and reeded wrought-iron and wooden furniture

GARDEN POTS AND ACCESSORIES

Andrew Crace Designs
Bourne Lane
Much Hadham
Hertfordshire SG10 6ER
Tel: 0127984 2685
Bronze garden ornaments, wooden furniture, hand-made oriental bamboo umbrellas, pavilions, pagodas, covered seats, obelisks

Avant Garden
77 Ledbury Road
London W11 2AG
Tel: 0171 229 4408
Wirework topiary forms, candle holders, wall sconces, candle baskets, terracotta pots

Clifton Little Venice
3 Warwick Place
London W9 2PS
Tel: 0171 289 7894
Wirework and ironwork baskets, chandeliers, topiary shapes, jardinieres, and replica stone urns, wall masks and fountain masks

Pots and Pithoi
The Barns
East Street
Turners Hill
West Sussex RH10 4QQ
Tel: 01342 714793
Handmade clay pots from Crete, including antiques

Traditional Garden Supply Company
(mail order catalogue)
Unit 12
Hewitts Industrial Estate
Elmbridge Road
Cranleigh
Surrey GU6 8LW
Tel: 01483 273366
Bird tables, nesting boxes, and other garden pet houses, plant stands, tools, accessories, small greenhouses and tool stores, plus a full range of garden practicalities such as composters, water butts, cold frames and work benches

Whichford Pottery
Whichford
Shipston-on-Stour
Warwickshire CV36 5PG
Tel: 0160884 416
A wide variety of handmade terracotta pots

GARDEN FURNITURE

Indian Ocean Trading Company
155–163 Balham Hill
London SW12
Tel: 0181 675 4808
Wooden furniture and benches, deck-chairs, steamers and garden umbrellas

Rusco Marketing
Little Faringdon Mill
Lechlade
Glouchester GL7 3QQ
Wooden and metal garden furniture, umbrellas and hammocks

AUSTRALIA

Amber Tiles
Tel: 132 241 for your nearest NSW store
Tiles, slates, pavers, terracotta

Cotsworld Garden Furniture Pty Ltd
42 Hotham Parade
Artarmon, NSW 2064
Tel: (02) 9906 3686
Imported teak furniture

Chris Cross
1575 Burke Road
Kew, Vic 3103
Tel: (03) 859 2666
Unusual landscape material

Elegant Garden World Pty Ltd
73–75 Market St
Condell Park, NSW 2200
Tel: (02) 708 5079
Pots, planters, fountains, birdbaths, statues, columns, balustrading, steps, paving, architectural monuments

The Lattice Factory
121 Church Street
Ryde, NSW 2112
Tel: (02) 809 7665
Design, make and install pergolas, fences, planter boxes – all made to measure

Materials in the Raw
Tel: 131 382 for your nearest Sydney store
Top quality landscape products, including decorator pebbles, pavers and treated pine timbers, plus imported pots and garden furniture

The Parterre Garden
33 Ocean Street
Woollahra, NSW 2025
Tel: (02) 363 5874
527 Military Road
Mosman NSW 2088
Tel: (02) 960 5900
New and antique urns and garden furniture

Porter's Original Paints
895 Bourke St
Waterloo, NSW 2017
Tel: (02) 698 5322
Manufacturers of fine paints

Whitehouse Gardens
388 Springvale Rd
Forest Hill, Vic 3131
Tel: (03) 877 1430
Statues, ponds, birdbaths, pots

CANADA

Cruikshanks Mail Order
Tel: 1-800-665-5605
Gardening supplies and accessories

Avant Gardener
2235 West 4th Avenue
Vancouver
British Columbia V6K 1N9
Tel: (604) 736-0404
Upscale garden accessories and garden statuary

Creative Wood Products
88 Shoemaker Street
Unit 1
Kitchener
Ontario N2E G4
Quality cedar furniture

Mason's Masonry Supply
6291 Netherhart Road
Mississauga
Ontario L5T 1A2
Paving supplies

INDEX

Page numbers in *italic* refer to the illustrations

ACKNOWLEDGMENTS

My thanks:
To *Debbie*, whose wonderful evocative photographs so brilliantly capture the very essence of "the decorated garden room", and for sharing with me an incredibly busy summer.
To all the contributors whose varied skills, creativity and talent have enriched the project element of the book.
To all the people who so generously let us photograph in their gardens, and whose infectious enthusiasm for gardening has enriched the design and plant element of the book.
To *Dominic Smith*, Hilltop Cottage, 9 Shirley Hills Road, Croydon, Surrey CR0 5HQ (tel: 01956 424021), who so meticulously designed and laid patios for us, and advised on and laid the flat bed for the Pretty Pebble Rug project.
To *Judith*, for coming back from maternity leave and so quickly grasping the character of the book, then skilfully guiding it into production.
To *Maggie Daykin* for being such a swift, sensitive and brilliant editor.
To *Lisa Tai*, designer, for bringing it all so beautifully to fruition.
And finally . . . to *Richard*, *Zoë* and *Faye* for being so patient through the summer in a house looking like a cross between a garden centre and DIY store, and *Debby*, *Christein* and *Mijke* who entertained the children so brilliantly while I gathered the material for the book.

CONTRIBUTORS

Cleo Mussi
Alpine Wheel, Miniature Pebble Circle, Pretty Pebble Rub and Mosaic Garden Table projects, and for lending her beautiful mosaic pictures, sculptures and pots.
Liz Wagstaff
Decorating a Shed, Stone-effect Wall Mask, Garden Console, Lead Chimney, Verdigris Bucket, Gilded Pots and Iron Lantern projects.
Karin Hossack
Tin-can Plant Nursery, Twigwam, Mexican Painted Pots, Chicken Box Plant Stand and Windchime projects, and the plant label plaque featured on page 124.
Jenny Norton
Painting the Customized Play House, painting the chairs on pages 96 and 97 and painting the wall featured on page 47.
Mijke Gesthuizen
Wire Heart project.

LOCATIONS

With many thanks to the following people, who very kindly let us photograph their gardens:
Bryan d'Alberg, Bill Blake and his gardener, Julian Hobbs, John Casson, Countess of Chichester, Mr and Mrs Eadie, Lucinda Ganderton, Ivan and Angela Hicks at The Garden in the Mind, Stanstead Park, Sandra Hanauer, Tony Hills at Wallace Antiques and Art, Sheila Jackson, Ann Kennedy of Agriframes, Lady Anne Rasch at Heale House Gardens, Diana Ross, Drummond Shaw of Drummonds of Bramley, and Gay Wilson.